Project
Teaching

Written by David Wray

4/7/02
A.Jw

Brig

Manag

Published by Scholastic Publications Ltd,
Marlborough House, Holly Walk,
Leamington Spa, Warwickshire CV32 4LS

© 1988 Scholastic Publications Ltd

Reprinted in 1989

Written by David Wray
Edited by Janet Fisher
Illustrated by Sarah Hedley
Designed by Sue Limb

Printed and bound by Richard Clay Ltd.
Bungay Suffolk

ISBN 0 590 70947 X

Front and back cover: designed by Sue Limb.

Contents

Introduction

Introduction

At one stage or another during their primary school life, most children take part in project or thematic work. This type of work varies a great deal; some teachers base almost their entire curriculum on it, while others arrange their work so that basic skills such as language, reading and mathematics are taught separately.

There are many ways of organising project work. For some classes, it is a whole-class activity, with all children simultaneously following the same line of work. In others it is an individual activity, and children are allowed to follow their own lines of enquiry.

Given the fact that project work varies so much, it is perhaps not surprising that it has raised an increasing amount of concern in recent years. This has been expressed over the relationship between project work and the concept of curriculum balance, particularly in the light of new developments in planning and the move towards a national curriculum. The content of project work and its effectiveness as a context for children's learning, has also been under discussion. Some people regard it as an opportunity for 'uninvolved copying', and doubt the extent of children's learning.

This book will try to show that concerns about the place and effectiveness of project work are unjustified, and areas such as curriculum continuity, planning projects, and how to use a range of resources will be discussed in detail. Also included are practical suggestions for organising and implementing project work in the classroom.

Throughout the book, emphasis is placed upon the role of children in project work. They should not just carry out the tasks planned and designed by their teachers, but should take part in planning, organisation and evaluation. Project work is not just a context for investigating a subject area, but is an opportunity for learning about learning, and for developing children's independence within it.

The first chapter looks at the reasons why teachers might choose project work as a teaching activity, and is followed by the process of planning projects and finding suitable starting points. The issue of curriculum coverage is discussed and the wide range of resources which a project may need are described with suggestions about how to store them, and ways of teaching children to use them effectively. The implementation of projects, ranging from different types of end-products to the teacher's role, are then examined. Finally helpful advice on techniques for evaluating children's achievements in project work are discussed.

The book's many practical suggestions are set firmly within an overall philosophy of involving children as much as possible in every stage of project work.

Chapter One

Why do projects?

So many doubts have been raised about the value of project work that teachers might be forgiven for wondering whether they should abandon this form of teaching and return to a more didactic, subject-centred approach. However, those who do favour a project approach need to determine carefully their aims and objectives for using project methods.

The aims of project teaching

As teachers, our aims are what we hope children will gain or learn from particular activities. We can divide these into three main types: those dealing with the knowledge or concepts children might learn; those concerned with the skills children might practise and develop; and those concerned with the attitudes which children might cultivate.

We will look at each of these aims separately but, firstly, let us consider the predominant aim of project work, that of building on children's interests.

Using children's interests

The most common advice given to student and probationary teachers who are concerned about how to manage their lively class of youngsters is, "Get them interested". Everybody knows that the more children are interested in what they are doing, the less likely they are to disrupt a class.

What is less well known is the fact that interested children, as well as behaving better, also learn better. Of course, it is possible to learn something without being really interested in it, as anyone who has ploughed through examinations will know. But this type of learning tends to become rote learning, and is soon forgotten. Learning about subjects which interest you, however, is much easier and you remember it for longer.

A simple test will demonstrate this effectively. Ask a group of junior school children to learn the following words which refer to types of birds: Menstilapicus, Ropidabicus, Formanichus, Disaltistin, Gretinumus. Some of the brighter children may manage it given time, lots of pictorial back-up and practice, but even these will probably forget the words by the following day. Try the experiment again, but provide the children with the names of types of dinosaur. Most seven-year-olds will not only know the words in a very short time, but will give you a full history of each creature by the next day!

Primary school teachers, on the whole, are a very privileged group. They deal with children who are, by their nature, interested in all sorts of things. In general, it is quite easy to interest primary children in worthwhile subjects.

This fact is of major importance and underpins the whole approach to project work.

As a short example, let us look at the simple skill of using alphabetical order to find items in a dictionary, a directory, or an encyclopaedia. Many teachers will testify that there are lots of children who find it difficult to master this skill. There are numerous exercises which claim to teach the skill, and while children dutifully complete these exercises, for many of them it seems to make little difference. Yet there are others who never do the exercises, but who pick up the skill simply by using encyclopaedias or dictionaries to find out more about subjects which interest them. The skill is therefore learned as a by-product of their interest in a particular topic.

This is the best justification for using the project approach. By focusing children's work on a topic in which they are already interested or in which their interest can be stimulated, a whole range of skills and concepts can be developed more easily than by direct teaching.

Developing knowledge and concepts .

The problem with facts

Many people judge the products of education by the amount of knowledge that has been acquired, and, indeed, this tends to be emphasised by public examinations. There are signs, fortunately, that this emphasis on facts may be waning. Many teachers now see that the development of skills and concepts is far more important.

The reasons for this shift in emphasis are not hard to find. We live in the age of the 'information explosion'. The amount of knowledge we have about our world is increasing so rapidly that it is becoming virtually impossible to select the vital facts that we consider children should

learn and remember. Any selection is arguable, as the world is in a constant state of change and progress.

Children all too soon forget most of the facts they pick up, unless, as argued earlier, they consider them to be of vital interest. As it really does not seem to matter which precise facts they learn in primary school, we might as well encourage them to learn those which interest them. In this way, they may at least remember what they learn.

Focusing on concepts

Concentrating less on facts does not, of course, mean that we can have no cognitive aims for project work. These aims should be concerned more with developing concepts rather than accumulating facts. As we shall see in a later chapter, project work can incorporate work in every area of the primary curriculum, and concepts appropriate to each area can be learned through projects. We can also integrate the curriculum so that concepts can be applied in several areas at once. The appreciation of cause and effect, for example, may have one set of implications in science work, but quite a different set in history.

It is possible to draft sets of key concepts for any area of the primary curriculum. The *Schools' Council 5-13 Science Project* (Macdonald Educational) covers the area of science; the *Schools' Council History, Geography and Social Studies Project 8-13* (Collins) covers the humanities. When planning particular projects you will need to draft your own set of concepts which you hope to develop, bearing in mind curriculum areas that the project will cover and the ability of the children.

Whose project is this?

Only from the teacher's point of view is the development of skills and concepts more important than the accumulation of facts. The children involved in the project will have completely different objectives. No child will respond positively if told that he or she is doing a particular project to develop their appreciation of causality and their abilities to use investigative skills!

Children's thirst for information is the key to the success of project work. This is not to say that children will not be interested and excited in doing tasks such as producing a collage or preparing their own video. But 'learning interesting things' will always be high on the list of what makes school worthwhile for a primary child.

There is therefore a clash of interests between how the teacher and the children view the purposes of project work. We must learn to teach the things

we consider important *through* the activities the children perceive as being important. This demands a certain type of negotiation with which most teachers may not be very familiar. We should be willing to explain to children why we want them to do certain tasks, and also be prepared to modify these activities in the light of how they react to them.

Developing skills

There is a whole range of skills which should be developed through project work. Some of these are only likely to be covered when doing a project, but all will be more effectively developed when children have a purpose to what they are doing. These skills can be taught through specific exercises, but in this way there is a danger of poor learning and inadequate transfer. Project work is particularly suitable for teaching certain skills.

Investigative skills

Most projects should try to include some first-hand experience for the children through which investigative skills can be developed. This could be outside the classroom, such as visiting an historical site. It can also take place inside the classroom, where objects can be handled or physical phenomena can be investigated.

Observation

Children can be very bad at noticing and looking closely at objects. They need encouragement to improve this skill. Children should be prepared so that they will know exactly what to look for.

To give one example, the project may involve a visit to a local woodland. One group may be asked to focus specifically on the various small animals they will see. They will look at pictures beforehand and discuss what they are likely to find. During the visit they may keep a log of what they see, noting any salient features which will enable them to identify the animals later. They may also make sketches or more detailed drawings where appropriate.

Identification
Children also need to be shown how to give names to what they observe. They will need to match features they have found with those described in other sources, and may have to use specific apparatus such as identification keys. In the woodland project example, the children may try to match their descriptions of the animals they

observed with those given in reference books on small mammals, birds and minibeasts. Younger children may simply note colour and shape, but older children will be able to use more sophisticated criteria.

Classification
Classifying phenomena into types is an important element of investigation and children need to be taught to pick out relationships with the things they observe. In the woodland project, the children could be encouraged to sort out the animals they observed into common sets. They may suggest several ways of doing this, perhaps beginning with colour and later moving on to the number of legs.

Recording
Observations will eventually need to be recorded although this need not worry

15

young children. There are many ways of doing this, which include drawing, painting, modelling, diagrams, writing descriptions, tabular forms, and so on. Each of these involves a set of practical skills which we will discuss later, but each also depends on what is being recorded and who will be using the information.

Explanation
Any investigation must include explanations. These must always be referred back to the subject to see if they hold true. This is the basis of problem-solving.

Practical skills
Here is a small selection of the practical skills which project work can develop.

Art and craft
Many forms of art and craft work, such as observational drawing, painting, collage, 3-D modelling, pottery and weaving are produced in the primary classroom. However, if they contribute to the presentation of a piece of project work, the children have a definite goal for acquiring and practising the necessary skills.

Using special apparatus
Apparatus such as magnifying lenses, microscopes, cassette recorders, slide viewers, video cameras, computers, overhead projectors and so on all have their place within the classroom. If the children are to use them efficiently and effectively they will need opportunities to practise the necessary skills. These opportunities may, of course, arise at any time and the novelty of the equipment may be enough to encourage them to learn to use it. The equipment will,

however, really come into its own when being used for a clearly identifiable purpose, and this is most likely to happen during project work.

Presenting information
Children need a range of practical skills to present information most effectively, including the ability to write legibly, and, perhaps, to enter information via a keyboard so that it can be printed out. They may also learn to bind their work into a book, and to acquire the basic knowledge of effective display techniques. Again, a project gives a real purpose to these skills.

Information and study skills
Project work plays a unique role in acquiring information skills. Finding and extracting information from appropriate sources is a part of most projects, and these often neglected skills can be developed in contexts which are real to the children. It is easy to see when they are weak in these skills. Those who leaf through reference books page by page, hoping to find by chance what they are looking for; those whose project work consists of sections copied word for word from these reference books; and those who, after the completed project, cannot tell you much about what they have learnt, are all likely to be weak in information skills. We can divide these skills into six sections.

Defining the subject and the purpose
Here we must specify what information is required and why. This implies more than the vague, 'I want to find out about . . .' which seems all too common in primary school information-handling work. Children need to be encouraged to specify, as precisely as possible, what it is

they want to find out, and what they will
do with that information when they have
found it. They may be asked to draw up a
list of questions requiring answers. This
at least will minimise the vagueness
which is a problem in much project work.

Locating information
Children must be able to find the
information they need in libraries, books
or elsewhere. They will need to know how
to use the library system to track down
likely sources of the information
required; how to find it efficiently in
books and other sources; and how to use
the most important resource — other
people.

Nor must we forget the various tools of
information technology which need
specific skills to extract information.
Teletext televisions, viewdata systems
such as Prestel, and computer databases
are all extremely useful sources of
information in the classroom, but only
when the children can use them
properly.

Selecting information
Children need to choose the specific
information they require.

Often they find it difficult to be
selective in the information they extract
from books in particular, and resort to
copying large extracts. They need to be
shown how to match their particular
requirements with what is available, and
how to note down facts rather than copy
them. Drawing up a list of specific
questions will certainly help them in this,
as they will then have to note down
answers to these questions rather than
everything quoted in the book.

Organising information
Pulling together information from a
range of sources can be a very
demanding task. It is, however, made a
good deal easier if the details needed are
defined precisely, as already suggested.
Children need to be encouraged to
consult a range of resources, and then to
look for common points or contradictions
in their notes.

Evaluating information
Children should be encouraged to evaluate the accuracy, relevance, and status of the information found. They tend to believe, as do many adults, that everything they read in books is bound to be true. The teacher may need to deliberately confront them with examples of incorrect or biased books in order to encourage a questioning mind. For this you could use out-of-date books, newspaper reports and advertising material.

Communicating results
The information gathered can be used either by the child individually or presented to others. If children have a definite audience for their work then they can assess the work's appropriateness by actually having it read. An example of this which immediately springs to mind is that of older junior children preparing booklets for younger children in the same school.

These skills have been described in terms of what a child may aim for by the end of the primary years. It is up to the teacher to set the finishing line. Children of any age can be introduced to information skills, as long as it is done in an appropriate way.

Communication skills
All types of teaching can appear to be concerned with developing communication skills. We are certainly familiar with the idea of developing language across the curriculum. Yet it is still probably true that most of the work children are expected to do in this area is done for its own sake, rather than having an express purpose. There is a place for language exercises, but the whole range of communication skills can be practised within a project without having to resort to particular tests. Communication, mainly, but not exclusively, concerns the 'language arts' (speaking, listening, reading and writing).

Oracy

The development of children's ability to speak clearly and appropriately is easier if they have something to speak *about*. Likewise they listen more attentively if there is something worth listening *to*. Project work can provide both of these opportunities.

During a project, children may have to ask people questions, hold interviews, listen to tape-recordings, tell and listen to stories, tell the rest of the class about their work, co-operate in small group discussions, and take part in improvised drama. All these activities will develop their oral skills, while simultaneously enhancing their work on a subject that interests them.

Reading

While working on a project children will be practising their reading skills without being aware of it. They will read reference books, stories, letters, advertisements, instructions, newspapers, wallcharts, as well as other children's writing. This provides a much wider variety of sources than a child's usual reading scheme work allows.

Writing

The same can be said about writing. There is, within project work, a great deal of scope for practice in most forms of writing: they include stories, poems, descriptive pieces, and personal reflections. Children can give reports, present arguments, record observations, and speculations. They can write for particular audiences and formats, and can be encouraged to draft and revise what they write. They can use pens, pencils, typewriters and word processors. All this vast experience can be provided with a real purpose — that of presenting

a piece of interesting work which their friends, classmates or others can share. This has a good deal more purpose than the common practice of working from exercise books, however well intended these may be.

Developing attitudes

Any classroom experience affects a child's attitude towards school and learning but, unfortunately, many children develop negative attitudes to the whole process. Nobody would claim that project work is a complete panacea for this, yet by interesting children in what they do at school you are likely to develop more positive attitudes. As suggested earlier, this is where project work's main strength lies.

Developing positive attitudes to learning

If we ask ourselves why negative attitudes towards learning develop, we might attribute most of the blame to two major causes. Firstly, what school may regard as suitable for learning may not coincide with the child's interests. Secondly, a child's experiences of school may include more failure than success and this will colour his or her whole perception of the process. Project work can, in favourable circumstances, work against both of these. Once a child's interest has been captured, it can result in all kinds of benefits, as the film *Kes* suggested powerfully. Encouraging children to *want* to know about something is the major part of the battle.

Kes also illustrated the negative effects which result from a child's perception of himself as a failure. The corollary of the old maxim 'nothing succeeds like success', is that 'nothing fails like failure'. By doing project work, it is possible, in a co-operative piece of work, for every child's contribution to be valued, and thus for every child to succeed to some degree. This, of course, demands sensitive handling by the teacher. Just because a child is good at making a collage he should not be asked to do this during every project. But there is scope in a project for whole groups to contribute to and take pride in well-produced work which will often go beyond their individual capabilities. 'The whole is often greater than the sum of the parts.'

Developing curiosity

Most young children are naturally curious about the world they live in. Sadly, for many of them, this will not be encouraged either at home or at school, and a great deal of potential may be lost.

Teachers therefore need to find ways of encouraging curiosity and the desire to enquire and to investigate. It would be very difficult to find an activity in the primary curriculum more suited to this than project work.

By its very nature, this revolves around 'finding out', and children can indeed make discoveries. It should be noted, however, that if this is to work it should be approached in a certain way. The teacher should not do all the thinking ahead of the children. This often happens, with the result that, far from developing curiosity, work is done through a series of teacher-devised worksheets. Clearly the teacher does need to pre-plan if the project is to be successful, but there must be scope left for children to follow their own leads.

Encouraging independence

It is often said that one of the aims of teachers is to make themselves redundant. If we are working towards the goal of child independence, there is little real benefit in teachers doing all the planning in project work by themselves. Children should be involved; if we do not let them make independent decisions, how will they ever learn to do so? Project work gives children the scope to develop their own lines of interest, to specify their own purposes, to find their own resources, and to decide how to present their own work. Of course the teacher should not opt out of helping, and the younger the children, then the greater the guidance they will need. But, wherever possible, the teacher should move towards being a guide rather than the source of all the answers.

Developing co-operation

Most teachers recognise the benefits of

encouraging children to co-operate in their work in all curriculum areas. They learn from discussing, sharing, and having to listen and to give their small contribution to something larger. Project work is ideal for this type of co-operation. Groups of children can work together with a single aim to produce a joint piece of work.

One of the criticisms often levelled at group work in primary schools is that it is not really group work at all. It is merely a group sitting close to each other, who happen to be doing the same work, but who make no attempt to co-operate. This problem arises because the nature of the task they are asked to do is more important to children than their seating arrangements, or their teacher's wish for them to collaborate. If their task is basically an individual one, they will not co-operate in a meaningful way. In a piece of project work, for example, a group's tasks can be defined so that the children are forced to co-operate.

Conclusion

Teaching would be a dull and sad affair if we were not allowed to have grandiose aims. We ought to have a reasonable idea of our aspirations in any kind of teaching, and these ought to be worth striving for.

Aims, however, are only a small but essential part of the story. We need to supplement them with some practical help. The following chapters will concentrate more on this practical guidance.

Chapter Two

Planning projects

The nature of planning

If project work is to fulfil its potential as a valuable part of the primary curriculum, and achieve some of the aims already outlined, it needs to be planned carefully. You will then have a clearer idea of exactly where the work is leading, and what children are learning in the process.

'Yes, but . . .', many teachers will say at this point, 'why is it that whenever I spend a long time planning something, it goes reasonably well but seems to lack sparkle, yet whenever I do something on the spur of the moment, it seems to go wonderfully well, the children are enthusiastic and produce work of a very high standard?'

Sometimes planning can be over-emphasised. Let us look more carefully at the reasons for this.

Planning as a framework
Does planning necessarily mean being prepared for every eventuality in teaching, to such a degree that nothing surprises or excites you? Well, of course, it *can* mean this, but this is not the impression I want to give. Here planning means thinking out a framework for events which might happen.

Within this framework we hope lots of exciting events will take place, with projects taking new directions depending on the circumstances and the responses of the children. Planning should allow for novelty, or it risks becoming a strait-jacket. It should not be thought of as a once and for all activity. Plans may be revised many times during the project, hopefully with the help of the children.

However, plans do need to be made. It is of little use spotting a wonderful opportunity to teach a particular skill, if you have to wait for the chance to make or collect suitable teaching materials. 'Strike while the iron is hot', is a useful phrase to bear in mind and your framework should allow for this kind of eventuality.

Who does the planning?
A second implication of the teacher's statement above is that projects seem more successful when they respond to children's enthusiasms than when planned beforehand. However, these two strategies are not mutually exclusive. Planning a project does *not* mean ignoring children's enthusiasm. On the contrary, it should use and develop it. Children should be consulted as much as possible in the planning process, so giving you the best of both worlds.

Essentials in planning
The main points you should bear in mind when you plan a project are to create a framework for possible lines of development rather than spelling out exactly where these lines should lead, and that the plans should involve the children from the very beginning.

Starting points

There are as many starting points to a project as there are projects, and only a few of the main ones can be mentioned here.

Visits
A class visit can be used very effectively as a stimulus point for project work. The possibilities are endless and vary from the spectacular to the everyday. Here are some suggestions with examples of the kind of work which the visit might stimulate.

A local farm
Children might study the kinds of animals to be found, the job of the farmer, the farming year, and the crops that are grown. They might compare different types of farms, in different parts of the country, and in different countries.

The railway station
The jobs of various railway staff might be studied, from engine drivers to station porters. Children could investigate the history of the railways, their local railway line, or how trains work.

The fire station
The job of the fire-fighter, fire-fighting techniques, and the sequence of events when a fire breaks out are all possibilities for work.

The local park
The ecology of the park could be studied, and flora and fauna mapped and investigated. Trees could be measured, identified and classified, leaf and bark rubbings made, and pollution indicators studied.

A castle or stately home
Information could be collected on the lifestyles of the former inhabitants. Children could write their own guidebooks to the building which would include mapping, measuring etc.

A zoo or safari park
Animals could be studied and comparisons made between their natural and present environments. The 'ideal' zoo could be planned and designed.

A museum
Children could design a 'museum trail' following a specific theme. Exhibits relating to the major theme of the project could be drawn and set in their historical context.

Local sports grounds
The history of local or national sports could be studied. Children could write their own sports rule books, either for existing or invented sports.

The supermarket
Types of goods could be surveyed, countries of origin mapped and tables of likes and dislikes drawn up. The children could examine certain items in more detail, for example, types of bread.

Factories of various kinds
Industrial processes could be studied along with the jobs that are done in the factory. Workers could be interviewed about their work and the factory's history researched.

The town centre
The town could be mapped, traffic surveyed, passers-by questioned about their destinations etc, and the results displayed graphically. Children could look at particular features such as one-way systems or shopping arcades and suggest improvements to their design.

Mountains, rivers, lakes, forests
Countryside visits have a good deal of scope for environmental study, perhaps focusing on flora, fauna, pollution etc. Recreational use of the countryside could be studied and children could design their own visitors' booklets.

A visit doesn't have to take place at the

beginning of the project. However, it is always a good idea to prepare children for what they might see by focusing their attention on a particular aspect or introducing them to a particular task. The prospect of going on a school trip will encourage the children to work hard. Preparing for a visit may take up more time than the follow-up work.

Visitors

Visitors from outside school can be a very useful stimulus to project work at whatever point during the work they come. One class of infants began an interesting circus project after a 'surprise' visit by a clown. More often, though, children will be prepared for the visitor, ready to focus on what he or she has to say, or to ask a set of questions.

Here is a brief list of some popular projects in which visitors could be involved. Often these will be ordinary people who simply come to talk about their jobs. If you can persuade your visitors to bring with them various objects of interest for the children to inspect or use, then so much the better.

People who help us
A popular project which could include a policewoman, a fire-fighter, a nurse, a postman etc. Often children's parents will fulfil one of these roles.

Transport
Maintain the human interest in what could become a mechanical project by inviting to your school an engine driver, a station master, a sailor (professional or amateur), a pilot, an air stewardess etc.

Communications
One class began a very successful project on films with a visit from a professional cartoonist. Other possibilities include a telephone operator, a postman, a photographer, a CB radio enthusiast etc.

Homes and houses
One top infant class working on a project on homes were lucky enough to have a parent who ran his own building business. He went to the school and gave them a demonstration of bricklaying, after which each child had a turn. Invitations could also go out to an estate agent, a beekeeper (bees have homes too!), or a policeman to talk about house security.

Dinosaurs
You could begin this popular project with a visit to a museum with dinosaur remains, but if this is impossible the museum curator might visit and bring to school some fossils, photographs and slides. You may know an amateur geology enthusiast who also has a fossil collection.

Music
Obviously a visit by one or more musicians will start this project off well. You may even be able to persuade a musical instrument maker to demonstrate his craft to the class.

Television/film
Many excellent projects have their origins in a television programme and there can be no doubt that television has a great deal of potential for stimulating children to produce interesting work. Television shows children, people and places that they could never see at first hand. Working with television in school may encourage them to watch television more actively when they are at home. A

29

video recorder is almost an essential piece of equipment to make the best use of television programmes with children. With a video you can watch a programme more than once, it can be stopped at any point for discussion, and groups of children can go back to sections they need to view again.

Film spools tend not to be used so much in schools now, having been almost entirely replaced by the video. Videos are more flexible and easier to use and I hope that all the excellent material previously available on film will eventually be transferred to video.

Slides/filmstrips
Like the television, slide collections give children a wider view of the world. However, for some children the still pictures are not as stimulating as the television. Slides are more flexible to use than filmstrips, as they can be used in a different order, or individually. I would recommend that you cut up and mount filmstrips as individual slides for this reason.

Stories/poetry
Stories and poetry are an often neglected starting point for project work. They are particularly useful as they act directly upon children's imaginations.

The class novel, which is told in serialised form over several weeks could form the basis of your project. Almost any children's novel is suitable to use, but particularly interesting projects have resulted from reading *Charlotte's Web* by E B White, *The Iron Man* by Ted Hughes, *The Sea Egg* by Lucy Boston, *The Third Class Genie* by Robert Leeson, *James and the Giant Peach* by Roald Dahl and *A Dog So Small* by Philippa Pearce.

You could choose several stories to fit certain themes and tell two or three each week. One example which worked successfully took the theme of animals and included the following stories: *The Elephant's Petals* by Brian Patten, *How the Whale Became* by Ted Hughes, *A Lion at School* and *A Hamster at Large,* both by Philippa Pearce. These were read to the children one a day for the first week, and each of the following five weeks concentrated on one of the stories, and one animal.

A one-off short story may be told several times. This approach requires particularly rich stories which could include: *Spit Nolan* by Bill Naughton, *Rikki-Tikki-Tavi* by Rudyard Kipling, *The Fib* by George Layton, *The Fantastic Machine* by Barry Maybury and many others by the same authors.

Read a long story—poem several times or in instalments to the children. Many ballad poems are suitable, such as *The Pied Piper of Hamelin* by Robert Browning, *The Lion and Albert* by Marriott Edgar, *The Golden Vanity* and *Lord Randal* (Anon) and *The Highwayman* by Alfred Noyes.

A single poem read several times over a period of weeks can also stimulate good project work. Most poems for children can be used in this way and a particular favourite is *The Marrog* by R C Scriven. (Full details of all the poems and stories mentioned here will be found in the Appendix, see page 123.)

Display

An interesting display of objects, pictures, books and stories will always be a useful accompaniment to any of the above techniques for starting a project. It may also be a good starting point in its own right. In this case it is probably best to set up the display and give the children a few days to look at, handle, and ask about its contents before attempting to introduce the project. Some children may wish to contribute to the display with objects from home, and this is a useful way of building up commitment.

Choosing and developing ideas

Almost all teachers, when starting a project off, will have some idea of the areas they hope to cover, even if these change and develop as the project progresses. There are several useful techniques available to help in planning these areas. In the next section we will discuss how the children can contribute to this planning. This section, however, concentrates on the teacher, and gives guidelines on various planning techniques.

Structuring plans
Most planning will begin with the teacher (hopefully in conjunction with the children) jotting down possible ideas as they come to mind. There are many sources of ideas from specially written books of project ideas, to children's workbooks, and teachers' magazines like *Child Education* and *Junior Education*. At this stage, don't evaluate the ideas which occur too rigorously, or bother to think them through. That can be done later. Concentrate on collecting ideas, and following the flow as one idea leads to another.

Having amassed a collection of ideas, the teacher can then go through the list, marking those which now seem impractical or unlikely. Don't discard them entirely yet, as you never know how things might develop; what may initially seem impossible might later be usable, perhaps in a modified form.

Checking curriculum coverage
At some stage you will need to sort out the ideas into the curriculum areas they cover. In this way you will be aware of the curriculum balance of the project. By doing this you may stimulate further ideas in curriculum areas which seem under-represented. Don't presume though that every project must cover all the major curriculum areas. This is probably impossible, and to attempt it is likely to lead to a great deal of artificiality. Some projects simply do not lend themselves to certain areas. On the other hand, there are some curriculum areas, for instance, language and creative arts, which seem to find a central place in every project.

You ought to be aware of the areas the project is covering for two main reasons: to check the areas which need extra work during the project, so that they are not neglected, and to try to ensure a balance in the type of projects undertaken during the course of a year. This may mean that one half-term's project which is largely based on environmental studies will be followed by a more 'mathematical' project.

The topic web
The topic web (often wrongly called 'flow diagram') is a very familiar project planning tool. It is a convenient way of linking ideas together. It may be designed simply to show how one idea links to another, or more formally, it might begin with curriculum areas from which appropriate ideas stem. For examples of each type see pages 34 and 35.

Further considerations
The topic web does not really go far enough in the planning process as it ignores many areas which need to be considered. We also need to think about what the end products of the project are

going to be, what resources we will need, how to organise the classroom and what deliberate teaching might be needed. Here is a checklist for further planning:

Outcome — what will be produced by the end of the project?
Format — what forms will this take? (Books, wallcharts, videos, tape-slide sets etc.)
Audience — who are the intended readers or users of the end products? (Children in the same, or different classes, younger children, other schools, local community etc.)
Resources — range: what kind of resources will be needed?
source: where will these be obtained from?
Organisation — time: how much time will be given to the project? (Half a term, whole term, one afternoon a week, half of every day etc.)
space: what areas of the classroom will be used for the project, either for working or display? (Project corner, topic table etc.)
classroom: how will the class be grouped for project work? What use will be made of whole class, group or individual work? Will project work be integrated into other

curriculum areas, and, if so, how?
Intervention — at what point in the project should the teacher intervene with direct teaching? (Skills or content teaching)
Evaluation — by teacher: when and how might the teacher evaluate skill and concept development?
by children: what opportunities might there be for children to evaluate their own or their peers' work?
by others: how might outside evaluation be brought into the project?
Keeping track — what records will be kept of individual, group or class progress?
We will discuss these issues later in the book.

Developing lists of goals
However long it takes to plan the project, you should aim for a very clear list of activities which the children will carry out in their groups or as individuals. If possible, the children should be provided with a copy of the list which clearly indicates which tasks *they* are responsible for. They can then tick off the tasks as they complete them. For examples from a project on holidays see pages 36 and 37.

Topic Web 1 — Idea focused

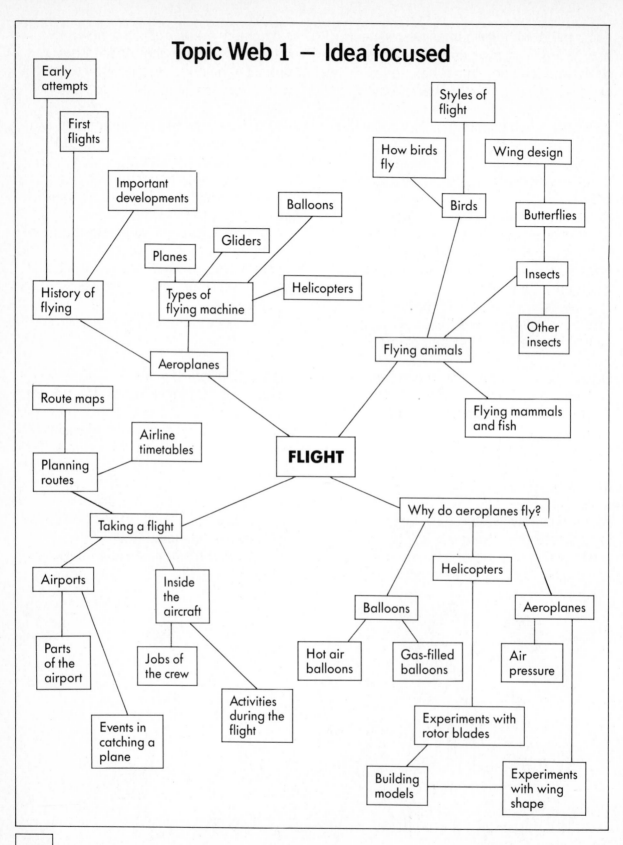

Early attempts

First flights

Important developments

Styles of flight

How birds fly

Wing design

Balloons

Gliders

Planes

Birds

Butterflies

Insects

Helicopters

History of flying

Types of flying machine

Other insects

Aeroplanes

Flying animals

Route maps

Airline timetables

FLIGHT

Flying mammals and fish

Planning routes

Why do aeroplanes fly?

Taking a flight

Helicopters

Airports

Inside the aircraft

Balloons

Aeroplanes

Parts of the airport

Jobs of the crew

Hot air balloons

Gas-filled balloons

Air pressure

Events in catching a plane

Activities during the flight

Experiments with rotor blades

Building models

Experiments with wing shape

Topic Web 2 – Subject focused

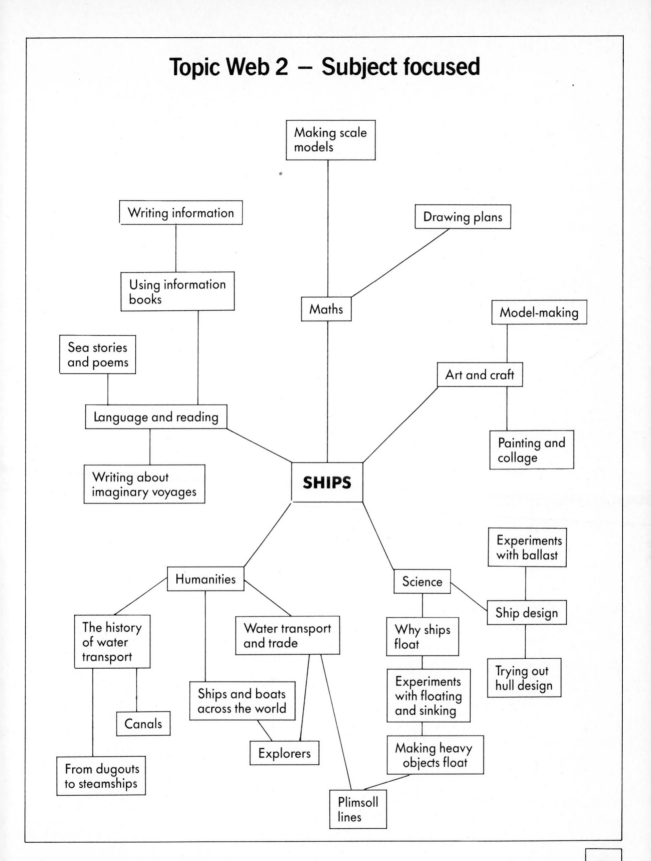

Holiday Assignments

1 Holidays

Write a story on 'The holiday of a lifetime.'

Collect a travel brochure from a travel agency. Choose a holiday from it.

Read all the small print and carefully fill in the booking form for the holiday you want.

Work out how much your holiday would cost your family.

Get a passport application form.

Fill it in.

Design your own passport (with correct number of pages, cover etc.)

Design your own travel brochure.

Make a checklist of things you would need to take on a holiday.

Make a list of questions a stranger might ask about the resort you have chosen for a holiday.

Use reference books to try to answer these questions.

Fill in the holiday questionnaire.

Tick if:

Needs written outcome	Your job	Done

2 Individual Topic

Choose a country you would like to holiday in.

Make a list of things you would like to find out about this country.

List a bibliography of all the books you are likely to need during your topic.

Survey all these books to find which are likely to be useful (check titles, contents, index and quickly skim through).

Plan your topic into sections. Your finished booklet should have about four or five chapters, each one describing a different aspect of your country.

Think of a way of recording which chapter each of your books would be most useful in. This will save you time.

Read your books to find the answers to your questions. Make notes as you read.

Write your findings up in *your own words*, in a booklet remembering to include:
1 Title page
2 Contents
3 Bibliography
4 Index

Done

Flexibility

Planning must be kept flexible, and allowance must be made for changes as the project proceeds. These changes might come about as the children become very involved in one aspect and wish to do more detailed work on it. There could be an unexpected event which provides an opportunity for a change in emphasis or the children could lose interest in one aspect, or lose their enthusiasm before expected.

You and the children can continually discuss what is happening and make changes, big or small, with the agreement of everyone.

Involving the children

The children's role in planning a project not only helps to ensure their enthusiasm for and their commitment to the project, but it also functions as a learning experience. Children will not always have a teacher on hand to plan their activities for them; at some stage they have to learn to do this themselves. Their role in the planning of projects can help them become more independent.

Negotiation

Obviously young children cannot immediately take over the planning of a project. Nobody would recommend that they get on with it by themselves. This is likely to lead at best to superficiality, and at worst to chaos. This is a learning process and the teacher should be involved all the time, guiding, encouraging and, occasionally, directing. Perhaps the best way of doing this is through negotiation. This means working alongside the children to help them to make decisions. At each stage of the project, the teacher should discuss with the children what is going to happen, listen to their ideas, contribute her own, and help them come to decisions which will be partly theirs, partly hers. This should concern as many of the details of the project as possible. For example:

- What activities will be included in the project?
- How will these activities be organised?
- What forms of grouping will be used?
- Who will be responsible for what?
- What resources will be needed?
- Where will these be obtained from?
- Who will get them?
- How will they be stored in the classroom?
- How will the furniture be arranged in the classroom?
- How will the display space be arranged?
- How much time will be devoted to the project?
- How will this time be used?
- How will everyone know what they are up to?

There are naturally limits on what children are capable of at various ages, but one thing is certain. If they are never given the chance to try, and sometimes to make a complete mess of the whole process, they will never become capable.

Strategies

Brain storming is often a useful technique to try at the beginning of project work. However, it can be hard work for the teacher, who has the responsibility of writing everything down. (Top juniors might just be able to manage this for themselves, but most younger

children will find it too difficult.)
Brainstorming involves everybody in the class or group contributing ideas as quickly as they can, with little initial attempt to evaluate their feasibility or suitability; this comes later. Try to use an overhead projector when writing down the ideas, as this allows ease of writing as well as letting the teacher face the class.

When sufficient ideas have been gathered (or the teacher is exhausted!) they have to be structured. If the session is concerned with ideas for what will be done in the project, the ideas will need to be grouped together according to similar features.

Grouping ideas into curriculum areas, as described in the previous section, will probably not mean much to the children, and is really a yardstick for the teacher. For the children the grouping will be more practical in that it will divide the project up into topic areas.

As an example of this, let us look at the process in action at the beginning of a class project on cars. A class of third year juniors watched an educational television programme about the development of the motor car, and brainstormed afterwards about activities they could do in their project. This is the resulting list. Items marked with * were contributed by the teacher:
Old cars
Racing cars
The first car
Rolls-Royce
Motorways
Car engines
Wheels
Highway Code*
Motor racing
Learning to drive*
Kinds of cars

How a car works
Roads
Lorries
Buses
Ambulances
Cars all over the world*
Car design

The next step was to sort the list out into topics. Together the class and the teacher rearranged the list as follows:

Old cars	Racing cars
The first car	Rolls-Royce
Car design	Kinds of cars
Wheels	Cars all over the world
Motorways	Car engines
Roads	How a car works
Highway Code	Motor racing
Learning to drive	Lorries
	Buses
	Ambulances

This gave six rough areas for the project with the general titles:
- The history and development of the motor car
- Types of cars
- Roads
- How a car works
- Learning to drive
- The uses of motor cars etc.

The class split themselves up, with some guidance and suggestions from the teacher, into six groups, each of which would concentrate on one of these topics. They then spent some time on further brainstorming sessions and structuring ideas for their own topics. The teacher arranged it so that this was done with her, one group at a time. This allowed her to add her own ideas to each group's topic, and to ensure that what they planned was feasible.

At the end of a week, each group had a

list of activities they hoped to do in their project, and allocated particular responsibility within the group. At the same time members of the groups were beginning to read about their topics and collect resources which gave them fresh ideas. Although a week seems a long time for planning, because little had actually been produced, much had been achieved. Each group had discussed their topic in general terms, had familiarised themselves with the areas to be covered, had a clear idea of what they were aiming to achieve, had clear individual responsibilities within the group's work, had worked out a rough time schedule for their work and had had their programme planned with the teacher to ensure that they would cover skills she felt them capable of and ready for.

Giving responsibility

One way that children learn to be independent is by being given responsibility for their own actions, and facing the consequences if things go wrong. This inevitably means that they will make many mistakes, but as long as they can learn from them, it can be a positive process. Of course, being given responsibility does not mean being left to flounder. Children are learning and they need the guidance of their teacher — as long as this gives them scope to make and live with decisions.

One example of this concerns a group of second-year junior children who were doing a project on flight. This group was responsible for work on the history of flight. Normally, the teacher planned the wall displays using the children's work. The group asked if, this time, they could have one of the display spaces and be allowed to plan and mount their own work on their topic. The teacher agreed somewhat hesitantly, expecting that her usual high standard of display would be let down. The end product, though, while not perfect by any means, was considerably better than she had expected. Thinking back she realised why. The children knew that they lacked their teacher's expertise in display, and at several points they had asked her advice, although they didn't always

accept it. They had decided she was a consultant, and had used her as such.

Another example concerns a mixed top infant/first-year junior class going on a trip to the local city farm as part of their project on animals. The children made all the arrangements for the trip, from informing the farm of their visit and its purpose, to booking a coach and working out the cost per child. Of course, the teacher had made all these arrangements beforehand, and had warned the various people to expect letters from the children. The class were unaware of this, however, and believed that the responsibility for arranging the visit, which they took very seriously, was entirely their own.

Resources and their access

While you plan the project, you should bear in mind the resources needed and how these might be made available to the children. We will now concentrate on those which are kept within the school, chiefly (but not exclusively) printed materials.

You must ensure that children have access to a wide range of resources. Here, however, is a simple checklist to help you plan as full a range of resources as possible:
- books,
- magazines,
- brochures,
- advertisements,
- pamphlets,
- forms,
- timetables,
- instructions,
- encyclopaedias,
- questionnaires,
- maps,
- dictionaries,
- computer databases,
- slide sets,
- cassette recordings,
- video recordings,
- stories,
- poems,
- posters.

Let's not forget the most important resource of all — people.

Access to school collections

For some resources it is only possible to keep a central school stock. If these are borrowed and kept in the classroom for the duration of the project, the rest of the school is unlikely to be able to use them. This applies especially to resources such as school library books.

A central stock of resources can create a problem of access for project work. Children will need to borrow items regularly from the central collection which means:

- the collection has to be organised so that they can find what they need without wasting too much time,

- they have to be taught how to find items in the collection,

- they have to be able to replace borrowed items in the correct place,

- they have to be able to use the collection without being under the direct supervision of the teacher.

If any of these conditions cannot be met, it does not mean that the children cannot use the central collection, but

that it is going to require more assistance from the teacher. Once or twice a week during the project, the teacher will probably need to accompany the class or group to the collection to help them find the resources they need. This, of course, can be a useful opportunity for teaching them to use the collection, so it may serve a valuable additional purpose.

For all their difficulties, centralised resource collections in schools are worth maintaining because:

• they permit a wider and more varied collection of resources,

• they can act as a model of the public library which children can thereby learn to use efficiently,

• they motivate teachers to teach their children to use them properly

(everybody soon complains when they get untidy and disorganised).

Class collections

Even if the bulk of books are kept in a central school library, it is useful for the class to have its own collection of heavily-used resources. This makes access easier and, for young children (perhaps eight-year-olds downwards) might be the only feasible way of ensuring that they use the books sensibly and well. You can easily supervise the use of class collections and prevent bad habits from being formed.

Class resource collections are often not properly organised. Because such collections are usually small, perhaps only 30 books or so, children can usually find the ones they want just by looking through them. This is, however, a bad strategy for researching information. With a small book collection, you can begin to teach good habits from the beginning. Make sure that the books are clearly organised in alphabetical order of authors' names, or, perhaps more usefully, into small subject areas. Give each book an identification number and/or colour, and display the key to these near the collection. Show the children how to use the system which can speed up their search for a book. When they go to a larger library, they will at least be familiar with the principle of library classification.

Perhaps you may borrow books from the county library service. In this case, you can reinforce the classification system by encouraging the children to help in sorting and organising the collection.

Resources from outside school
Resources from outside school can add a more adult, realistic flavour to the project, and can also develop children's independence in acquiring sources of information. Some examples of this type of resource are:
- holiday brochures,
- telephone directories,
- advertising leaflets,
- application forms of various kinds,
- instruction leaflets,
- notices,
- magazines,
- timetables etc.

These and other similar items can be used in a variety of projects. If you bring them into class yourself, a valuable opportunity will be missed. Let the children collect the items themselves. If you discuss beforehand, and delegate the children to acquire these items, they will learn a great deal about information in the adult world.

As an example of this, in a project on holidays one group of six children

'persuaded' their parents to take them to various travel agencies to collect holiday brochures. Two children borrowed their parents' passports so that the rest of the class could make their own copies and all the children acquired passport application forms from local post offices. Half the class brought to school their families' out-of-date Yellow Pages telephone directories. Most of the class wrote off to various tourist boards for information and several children visited the local railway station's information office and collected timetables and publicity materials.

The physical context

When deciding on the layout of the classroom, the main concerns are how the furniture should be arranged, how resources should be arranged and displayed, and how the work resulting from the project should be displayed. You should also decide on how much time to devote to the project. Once again, you should consult the children about all these matters.

Arranging the classroom
In most classrooms no special arrangements need to be made to accommodate work on a project. However, if one of the aims of the project is to develop children's ability to work co-operatively, then the arrangements of the furniture will have to be discussed. Few primary classrooms have all the children permanently sitting in rows facing the front of the class. This is the best way of arranging the class if you

have to present material to all the children. It is less effective, however, when the children are discussing and producing their work together and on these occasions the familiar groups of tables are more appropriate.

When children are working on a project, they often have several books and other resources in front of them, as well as their note books and project folders/books. This means that they need more working space than usual and it is a great help if they can 'spill over' into other areas. A few extra tables set up somewhere in the classroom, say as a project corner, will accommodate this. Some children may be quite happy working on the floor. You will inevitably have to accept a much more flexible physical arrangement than the 'one child/one desk' system. Such flexibility will demand greater organisational skills than usual and a greater awareness of everything which is going on in the classroom.

Finally, you should consider how children might work together on large items, such as wallcharts, or friezes which demand large spaces for the work to spread out. One solution is to use a corridor or hall, but if this is not possible, rearrange the furniture in the classroom to provide an appropriate space.

The arrangement of the classroom needs to be a good deal more flexible for project work than for most other activities. It may need to change from lesson to lesson, and, unless the children are prepared and trained to do this without fuss, it can rapidly become wasted time.

Space for display
Most projects will generate a lot of work which can be displayed for others to see. Indeed, the display will often be the main aim of the project. Unless your classroom walls are conveniently made from pin-board, finding a space to display work can be a problem. While you plan the project, try to ensure that children are not going to produce work which cannot be displayed for lack of space. This would be really disheartening.

Here are some points to consider.
• There is little point in displaying children's written work above their eye-level. If other children cannot read it, it is wasted.

• If space on the walls is at a premium,

consider extending it by using: rolls of corrugated cardboard; 3-D displays with writing on cards or zig-zag books which stand up; mobiles made from plastic hoops, from which writing and pictures can be hung, and inn-sign displays on which writing can be hung.

• Three-dimensional displays usted cardboard; 3-D displays with writing on cards or zig-zag books which stand up; mobiles made from plastic hoops, from which writing and pictures can be hung, and inn-sign displays on which writing can be hung.

• Three-dimensional displays using covered tables always look effective.

• Don't forget that displays are best thought of not as art galleries before which you stand and admire, but rather as developing collections which reflect the work children are doing, and stimulate further work.

Displaying resources
As we discussed earlier, you need to give some thought to the arrangement of resources so that they are easily available to the children. Some will probably form part of an initial display around the project, while others can be given a shelf or two to themselves. Consider displaying them in two or more parts of the classroom since this will reduce the crush as all the children try to find books at once. Clear labels will help children to know exactly where to go, and where to return books when they have finished with them. Appoint some children as resource monitors, with the job of ensuring that everything is put back tidily in the correct place at the end of each session.

Allotting time
The amount and the frequency of time that is allotted to project work varies greatly. Often it reflects the importance given to it. It is quite common for only one or two afternoons a week to be devoted to projects. In this case the message is clearly that projects are an extra in the curriculum and do not have too much importance.

For it to be taken seriously project work needs more time, and certainly time of higher status, that is, mornings as well as afternoons. There are classrooms in which the entire week is spent on project work, and all curriculum work is integrated into the project. This is probably too much for most teachers.

Less extreme, perhaps, is the integrated day approach, in which throughout most of the day, some children, but not the whole class, are doing project work, while others work on different tasks. This approach can allow the teacher to spend her time flexibly and usefully, working with small groups and individuals where necessary. There is no single ideal way of allocating

time to project work, and this will, in any case, differ from project to project. Sometimes it may be appropriate to devote an entire week to a project and then do no more for the next month. At other times, a regular day, or day and a half, spread over half a term may be better. Teachers will, of course, decide for themselves, but bear in mind that chidren will usually value the things their teacher obviously values, and they are very adept at perceiving which activities are really valued in their classroom.

The social context

Grouping children for project work is an important task. You need to consider how to use particular talents to the best effect, and still ensure all-round development.

Grouping
By putting children into groups the whole class need not be simultaneously involved in the same tasks. This is a good use of resources and teacher time. Group work also provides the potential for a great deal of learning through discussion. It is well to notice, however, that there is often less discussion than you might hope for because the children in the group simply get on with their individual work rather than co-operate. This is largely the fault of the kind of tasks they are doing. If you want them to learn through discussion, then the tasks they do must require discussion, that is, they must be joint tasks. If the group has to co-operate to produce a single end-product, they have to discuss it as they go along.

The size of the group will influence the benefits children receive from working in this way. If the group is too big, they will not all get the chance to contribute. Six is probably a maximum size, unless they are working on a very large task. Neither must the group be too small, as this places too much responsibility for generating ideas onto too few children. Don't have less than three children in a group.

Take care too in selecting the group. For some tasks a group of children of similar ability might be better, but for others, a mixed ability group might bring out the best in all its members. Be flexible and relate the grouping to specific activities.

Using particular talents
Children with special talents can come into their own in project work. Not only can they contribute their speciality to their group work, but they may also act as 'consultant' to the rest of the class for particular tasks. There will for example be children with knowledge about computers, or railway trains, or who have musical abilities which can be used by the whole class. A child will also increase in self confidence as he shows his talent.

All-round development
Children with special talents do not have to spend all their time using them, at the expense of doing other things. This would prevent them from developing other equally important abilities and would deprive other children of the opportunity to practise and learn skills which come easily to these certain children. For this reason, the 'consultancy' approach is preferable to the specialist approach. 'Consultant' children help others and themselves at the same time.

Chapter Three

Curriculum

Problems

' "Miss Beale said you would show me round, to look at the projects,' said Andrew.

"Why, do you want to copy one?" asked Victor. . . . "You could copy mine, only someone might recognise it. I've done that three times already."

"Whatever for?" said Andrew. "Don't you get tired of it?"

Victor shook his head and his hair.

"That's only once a year. I did that two times at the junior school and now I'm doing that again," he said. "I do fish, every time. Fish are easy. They're all the same shape." '
(from *Thunder and Lightnings* by Jan Mark)

Many teachers will, perhaps somewhat guiltily, recognise Victor's experience of project work. Is it possible for children to repeat the same project several years running? The answer too often is 'Yes', simply because we have not solved the problem of continuity. The problem may also arise in another way. The HMI survey report, *Primary Education in England* (published by HMSO, 1978) commented on the lack of continuity between projects within particular classes. Referring to historical topics, they found that, 'In some classes children moved from one assignment to another in a fairly random way so that work on Ancient Greece might immediately precede or even follow a study of 'travel in Stuart times'. They refer to 'a fragmented approach', and comment that work shows 'little evidence of progression'. Clearly this is a real problem and, if project work is to fulfil some of its great promise, continuity and curriculum coverage need to be considered.

What is the primary curriculum?

Let us first briefly examine the primary curriculum. Debates about it have already filled many books and journals and no doubt will continue to do so in the light of the forthcoming Education Reform Act. Nevertheless, there appears to be a large consensus among teachers and schools about the content of the primary curriculum.

A 'national' curriculum has, in fact, been operating in most primary schools for many years. All primary schools give great attention to the teaching of reading, to children's use of language, and to mathematics, even if they vary considerably in how they teach the subjects. Schools also recognise the importance of science, religious education, study of social and environmental topics, physical education and art and crafts, although the amount of work done in these areas varies.

There is, of course, major debate about how these subjects should be taught, and about the amount of time that should be devoted to each of them. Although greater national conformity over curriculum time allocation is perhaps desirable, it is very unlikely that any rigid rules will be imposed upon teachers about *how* to teach elements of

a nationally agreed curriculum, if only because of the sheer diversity of teaching methods now in use.

One of the major areas under discussion which concerns the role of project work, is the issue of integration. This has been debated by those who believe that the primary curriculum can be treated as a collection of subjects, and those who see it in terms of a 'seamless robe of learning'. Most teachers now accept that rigid subject divisions are artificial for primary school children and do not reflect the way young children see the world. Many, however, are wary of abandoning subject divisions entirely, and are concerned about external pressures, and demands for 'standards.'

Project work can fit into either of these categories. Projects can be planned so that all class work relates, for a time, to the project being undertaken. They can also be planned so that, at different times during the week, children study historical aspects of the project, geographical aspects, scientific aspects and so on. You can also plan a project around certain subject areas only, leaving others to be studied at separate times.

Whichever of these approaches is taken will tend to reflect an individual teacher's feelings about curriculum integration and its feasibility. It must not be forgotten, however, that by using project methods at all implies a certain acceptance of the concept of an integrated curriculum. Any method of approaching a project will hopefully enable children to see links between the various pieces of work they do, in an attempt to remove some of the artificiality.

The debate in project work will not be about *whether* the curriculum should be integrated, but rather to what extent. To clarify the issues, we need to look at some of the possibilities for placing project work in the curriculum.

Project work within the curriculum

Many teachers tend to see the curriculum in terms of 'skills and frills': that is, composed of certain essential, basic parts, and other less essential, more informal parts. At present, the curriculum is divided into the formal and the informal, the former consisting basically of the 3Rs, and the latter, subjects such as art, PE, environmental studies etc.

Some teachers regard project work as an opportunity to teach 'basic' subjects in a more meaningful and interesting way, and it therefore becomes a basic part of their curricula. Others see it as an extra and an opportunity for children to practise basic skills which have been taught elsewhere. To others, it is still

seen as a motivating extra, but they deliberately structure the project and their basic skills work so that the two interact. These three approaches result in different ways of planning and executing project work.

Projects and basic skills

The integrated approach
In this approach the teacher uses the project as a vehicle for teaching basic skills. By using this method, the teacher believes that such skills can only really be learnt if the children see for themselves that they are useful, and if they are set in a practical, purposeful context from the beginning. One objection to this approach is the incidental nature of such teaching and the possibility that opportunities to teach certain skills may not occur naturally. This may result in certain areas being missed and/or insufficiently developed. We can counter this objection by taking two initial precautions.

51

Firstly, we can draw up a programme for the teaching of basic skills which can help to ensure full coverage over a certain period. This programme is likely to be more effective if it is planned on a whole-school basis, and if it is accompanied by a form of record-keeping. Secondly, in implementing this approach, extra basic skills teaching can be planned, both to 'top up' that already done during the project, and to cover areas which it may not be possible to integrate.

This example may help to clarify this approach. In a project on holidays with a mixed class of third- and fourth-year juniors, the teacher drew up the following list of basic skills (covering elements of all the 3Rs) which it was hoped could be learned during the project:

- Reading for details,
- Reading critically,
- Surveying books and other written,
- materials,
- Using reference books and encyclopaedias,
- Using telephone directories,
- Writing letters,
- Writing narrative,
- Writing to persuade,
- Writing to describe,
- Writing personally,
- Reading and making maps,
- Measuring distances and using scale,
- Performing calculations with money,
- Using timetables.

When planning the project (with the children) the teacher deliberately included activities which would exercise and so teach the skills outlined above.

Reading for details
Reading reference books and holiday brochures for details of specific resorts and countries. Reading brochures for details of prices and conditions of holidays (small print). Reading application forms for passports.

Reading critically
Reading holiday brochures and other publicity materials for the truth about resorts and hotels etc.

Surveying books and other written materials
Checking a variety of written materials to ascertain whether they contained useful information. Using contents and index pages of books. Skimming printed materials quickly.

Using reference books and encyclopaedias
Looking for information about countries and cities in the world, specifically concerning their tourist attractions. Finding out about various holiday pursuits, eg canoeing, swimming, windsurfing etc.

Using telephone directories
Finding phone numbers and addresses of local travel agents. Finding suppliers of certain holiday goods.

Writing letters
Writing to tourist offices to request information.

Writing narrative
Writing accounts of holidays, real and imaginary.

Writing to persuade
Writing holiday brochures to advertise particular resorts.

Writing to describe
Writing descriptions of holiday resorts, holiday activities and experiences.

Writing personally
Writing personal reactions to places visited on holiday, or about experiences.

Reading and making maps
Using maps of the world and Ordnance Survey maps to locate countries and resorts, and to plan routes. Making maps of various scales to show places visited and written about.

Measuring distances and using scale
Working out distances to, and between resorts on the maps used, and converting these using scales of the maps.

Performing calculations with money
Working out the cost of holidays from various brochures for their particular families. Working out deposits, insurance, and travel costs.

Using timetables
Working out travel times for journeys to various resorts, using rail, bus and air timetables.

While children were engaged in these activities, the teacher took the opportunity to teach children directly the appropriate skills, using as a starting point the materials arising from the project. It was felt, however, that some skill areas were missing from this work, and these were given teaching time independent of the project work. These areas were:

● Reading for pleasure (this occupied a regular half-hour slot every day).

● Extra basic reading help for those with difficulties (using their usual readers, although several lessons included reading material from the project).

• Basic maths computational practice (using the school's usual maths scheme).

• Science work which was found difficult to fit into holidays, but concentrated during the period of the project on water, which seemed as near as could be achieved!

The sequential approach

Here, project work is regarded as an opportunity for children to put to purposeful use the basic skills they have already been taught. Project work, therefore, has to follow basic skills work and thus be separate from it. This approach has several implications. Because basic skills are taught in time defined by the teacher, the children will sense that this is the work that the teacher really considers to be most important. They will begin to realise that project work is less important, and hence less worthy of real effort. The teacher will have to work very hard to make them see it as a vital and interesting activity — the only way of providing a motivating context in which to practise basic skills.

With this approach there is a gap between the teaching of a skill and its use in a project. By the time they come to the project, there is a chance that children will have forgotten some of the basic skills. It is even more likely that they may not be able to transfer their skills from one context to another. Children can spend long periods learning spellings for a test, only to misspell the very same words when writing a story. In project work it may be found that children who can successfully complete any amount of exercises on study skills seem to forget all their knowledge when they come to use reference materials in earnest. Transfer of learning can be a real problem.

Because of these inherent problems, it is unlikely that this approach will satisfy

the aims of those who use it, or be an effective use of project work.

A compromise approach may be welcomed by those who wish to avoid the problems discussed, yet feel hesitant about adopting the all-or-nothing fully integrated approach.

The concurrent approach

Those who use this method try to teach basic skills alongside their use in project work. The skills can therefore be taught systematically and in the structured way many teachers are familiar with. Children also have opportunities to use the skills in real contexts and for real purposes as they learn them. This hopefully avoids the problems of children forgetting or being unable to transfer skills.

To show how this approach can work, let me give you an example of part of a project on aeroplanes undertaken by a class of first and second year juniors. The teacher decided that the children would need to use the following skills:

- Reading to pick out the main ideas,
- Summarising in their own words,
- Handling reference books (using the contents page),
- Writing to communicate information,
- Arranging in order of size,
- Drawing to scale.

In groups, the children had to make booklets about famous aeroplanes. This would require all the above skills to be used. They had to find information about various aeroplanes in reference books, noting down the main points about each one, and compiling it into a page or two about each plane. When this was done, they had to arrange the planes in order of length, attach a drawing of each on roughly the same scale and make up

their booklet which would then be displayed for the rest of the class to read.

The teacher began with some work on finding information in reference books. Two or three lessons on this finished with exercises for the children to do in groups and by themselves. After these she introduced the reference books on aeroplanes and held a series of group lessons (because there were not enough books to go round) on their use. The children were then asked to find and read the sections of the books on the planes they wished to study.

While they were doing this in their groups, alongside other normal classwork, the teacher began some classwork on note-taking. After several exercises she asked the groups to note down items of interest about the aeroplanes. The next step was to ask them to write from their notes, and this was similarly introduced and practised by the whole class before being carried out as part of the project. The work continued like this, with skills being introduced and practised, as far as possible, by the whole class, before being used in the project.

While this approach may seem to combine the best of both worlds, having both structure and purpose, it does demand a great deal of forethought and planning. It is unlikely that approaching every project in this way could be sustained for long. As children differ in their ability to learn new skills, the class teaching elements as described in this example become ineffective and the teacher will need to concentrate on more individual or group work. However, this approach does have much to commend it, and it is certainly recommended if the teacher finds it feasible.

Project work and the informal curriculum

Most teachers accept that project work is an ideal vehicle for teaching subjects such as art and craft and environmental studies. Art and craft may well feature on the timetable as a separate subject, but its content will often be related to current projects.

We must remember, however, that the children's experience of these subjects should not be confined to simple practice. Each area of the curriculum has its own particular skills which need to be given attention. The skills of an area such as environmental studies overlap with those specified in Chapter One. If we remember that these need deliberate teaching, then project work is the obvious context for this.

The many skills involved in the field of art and craft can pose problems. Often these are not taught at all, and children are expected pick them up by practice. Thus children may be asked to paint, draw, or make a model and are then left to their own devices. The necessary skills are not built up, and the end result is that certain children become known as 'natural artists', while others regard themselves as being 'no good at art'. The systematic teaching of skills can avoid much of this, and, again, project work can provide an ideal opportunity in which to teach them.

Curriculum balance

Many studies of practice in primary schools have shown a wide variation in the amount of time devoted to specific curriculum areas. In terms of hours per week, mathematics may be given anything from three to twelve hours in different classes. If we accept that children can only learn what they are given an opportunity to learn, there is clearly a case for attempting to standardise curriculum time, even though we would wish to leave something to the teacher's discretion. Individual teachers also have to consider how they might achieve a balanced curriculum for their children, whatever the content of that may be.

Project work may take up a large slice of the time in a primary class, but its impact on curriculum balance must be considered. The integrated nature of most project work makes this a little difficult, but some attempt needs to be made by the teacher to weigh up how much of the work of particular projects is devoted to the various curriculum areas.

In order to do this, we need to decide on what the key curriculum areas are. This can be a very difficult issue since there is no complete consensus between the many analyses of the curriculum which have been published. As a starting point, you may find the following table useful. You can decide exactly how far you want to sub divide each area. The four basic curriculum areas are listed on the left and sub divided on the right.

If you take the level of sub division you prefer, and then try to decide on the amount of time likely to be spent by children on each of these areas during an average week's work on their current project. To these figures, add the time devoted specifically to the areas elsewhere in the week. This will give a rough and ready measure of current curriculum time allocation. It is up to you then to decide whether this is what you want, or whether it adheres to curriculum guidelines, either local or national.

Language

Reading

    Learning to read
    Reading to learn
    Reading for pleasure

Writing

    Writing for various purposes
    Writing for different audiences
    Physical and technical aspects

Oral work

    Speaking
    Listening
    Discussion

Maths

Number

    Using concrete experiences
    Developing abstract ideas

Shape

    3-D
    2-D

Practical

    Measuring
    Investigations

Discovery

Environmental

    Local geography
    World geography
    Investigations

Social

    History
    Social studies
    Religious studies

Scientific

    Experiments
    Observations
    Recording

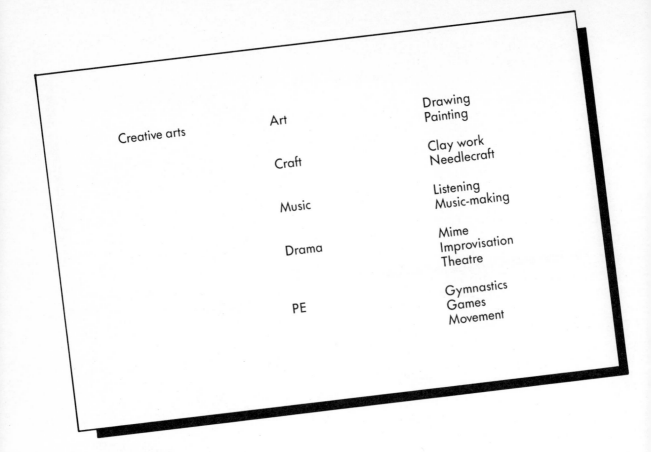

Creative arts

Art — Drawing / Painting

Craft — Clay work / Needlecraft

Music — Listening / Music-making

Drama — Mime / Improvisation / Theatre

PE — Gymnastics / Games / Movement

If you don't achieve a fair balance (and you are unlikely to, simply because you have analysed only one week of the year, which may not be typical), you then need to consider how to improve it. The following strategies for handling imbalance relate particularly to project work.

• Check whether it is possible to alleviate the imbalance by adjusting the time given to various areas outside project work time. This may involve replacing a language session with a maths session, or planning a regular science session, for example.

• Is it possible to add extra dimensions to the project work to make up for lack of coverage of certain areas? Is it possible, for instance, to think of a way of bringing maths work into the project (always bearing in mind the dangers of artificiality discussed earlier)?

• Make a note that in the next project certain areas may need to be at the forefront so as to compensate for their lack of coverage in the present one. Thus a science-based project might be followed by one with a high literature content. Balance may be achieved over a whole term or year, rather than every week.

Curriculum continuity

If a child repeats a project in two different classes, this does not necessarily mean that the second attempt has been a waste of time. The concept of the 'spiral curriculum' suggests that similar topics can be studied at various stages with, on each occasion, the children gaining fresh insights and a fresh depth of understanding. To repeat something can be a very valuable learning experience for children. Consequently, simplistic views about continuity, which specify suitable content for particular age groups, may actually work against potentially useful learning.

The specification of suitable project titles for particular age groups has become a popular response to the problem of continuity. A school might develop a list such as the following:

Suggested projects

Age group	Possible project themes
6+	Animals
	Homes
	Our street
	Prehistoric animals
7+	Early man
	Farming
	Shops
	The sea
8+	Explorers
	People who serve us
	Water
	Our town
	Romans
9+	Food
	Weather
	Communications
	Space
	Normans
10+	Europe
	Elizabethans
	Transport
	Our bodies
	Victorians

Such a list has the advantage that suitable resources for each project can be centralised, ideas for development can be passed on from teacher to teacher, and, if the list is a product of detailed staff discussion and is reviewed regularly, it can be a useful means of ensuring continuity. However, there are several inherent problems:

• Children may not have the opportunity to develop and extend their learning in certain areas over longer periods than the duration of a single project. So their learning through projects risks becoming like a series of snapshots, which are difficult to relate one to another.

• By concentrating on titles, there is a risk that project work will emphasise content over processes of learning and skills.

• By specifying titles for projects, teachers' enthusiasm and intiatives take second place to a predetermined plan. Teachers may find several of the suggested titles for their age group are unstimulating, and if a teacher is bored by a subject, so the children will be.

• Finally, and perhaps most importantly, the system does not allow for children's interests, or for events which may occur without warning, yet still provide scope for wonderful projects.

To achieve continuity, there are two alternative approaches to the pre-determined list of titles. One relies on simple record-keeping procedures. If teachers keep records of the projects that individual children have done under their supervision, these can be passed to the next teacher, along with, if possible, samples of work from each project. The new teacher can then decide whether to use completely new topics for project work, or whether to build on work the children have done in the past.

The second alternative regards continuity more in terms of developing skills and concepts than in covering content. We shall look at this in more detail.

Mapping objectives

There has been much debate over setting out objectives which children should be expected to achieve by certain ages. If objectives are seen in terms of skills and concepts, the approach has its attractions. Teachers can know what skills and concepts to concentrate on with their classes, and what to evaluate and record. Continuity depends to a large extent on the sequential development of skills and concepts, and without guidelines it is difficult to see how teachers can ensure their children are making progress, rather than marking time or regressing. However, there are several problems with this approach to continuity which need further discussion.

Firstly, a list of specified objectives should not be seen as a strait-jacket. There is no such thing as the perfectly average class or child, and consequently any set of objectives must be at least partially inappropriate for any group of children. The most important factor in what any teacher can achieve with a class is, of course, the children themselves, and they will largely determine the feasibility of any pre-specified objectives. So in any class, there may be children who will be able to achieve more than is anticipated in the objectives, and there will certainly be those for whom the objectives are over-ambitious. The teachers will constantly need to readjust expectations in the light of experience with particular children.

Secondly, appropriate objectives vary from school to school, and no single set will fit exactly the needs and potentialities of any two schools. Because of this it is essential that lists of objectives are tailored to particular schools. The staff of each school must work together to devise their own objectives, even if they use a list derived from elsewhere as a starting point.

Objectives should also be seen as processes which children should experience. The process/product debate has a long history in education, and the concept of objectives for learning has tended to be seen in product terms. If we regard objectives as specifying processes, we may use terms such as, 'Children should have experience of using a book to search for information', rather than, 'Children should be able to use a book to search for information'. The latter does not specify any particular conditions under which this should be judged, such as the difficulty of the book, the motivation of the child, the purpose of the exercise etc, all of which can affect the child's ability to do the task. It would, therefore, be very difficult to say that a child had achieved this objective. Yet we can say that a child has had experience of something, without having to make dubious judgements about the success of this experience.

Lastly, objectives do not provide teaching material in their own rights. In specifying objectives, teachers might feel they have to teach them directly. This can result in teaching which has little real meaning for the children. Any teaching needs to be set in a meaningful context if it is to be fully effective. Thus objectives should inform teaching rather than determine it.

If these points are remembered, details of objectives can provide useful guidelines for the teacher. There are several sources of such objectives. On pages 62 and 63 is one list which consists of the skills of information handling which were agreed by one junior school as being the focus of each year's work. The list is aimed at the 'average' child, and should be interpreted very flexibly.

The handling of information

First year juniors
- Putting words into alphabetical order using the first letter.
- Using the first letter to find a word in a dictionary or encyclopaedia.
- Using a simple dictionary to check the meaning of a word, or its spelling.
- Finding a book on a particular subject by searching the shelves.
- Using features of the book such as title, cover, and publisher's blurb to determine the subject.
- Using the contents page to locate specific chapters.
- Reading for main ideas eg reading a chapter in order to give it a title.
- Finding specific facts in a book by scanning.
- Writing the information gleaned from a book in one's own words.
- Choosing appropriate pictures to illustrate what has been found out from books.

Second year juniors
- Consolidation of first-year skills.
- Using second and third letters to put words into alphabetical order.
- Finding words in dictionaries and encyclopaedias by second and third letters.
- Using the volume titles of encyclopaedias to find correct volume eg ABLE to AXE.
- Using guidewords to find words in a dictionary or encyclopaedia.
- Opening a dictionary at roughly the correct place to find a word.
- Using the subject index to find the Dewey number of a subject.
- Finding the shelf with the correct Dewey number and picking out a relevant book.

- Assessing the usefulness of a particular book by glancing through it.
- Using an index to find specific facts.
- Using a glossary to understand difficult words.
- Reading a book to answer specific questions.
- Checking the information found in one book by reading another on a similar subject.
- Using the information found in a book to write imaginative stories.
- Presenting information by charts or diagrams where appropriate.
- Compiling a list of books used in a particular investigation (bibliography).

Third year juniors
- Consolidation of first and second year skills.
- Using a thesaurus to find words of similar meanings.
- Understanding the dictionary treatment of multi part words eg football, foot-pump.
- Using cross-references in an encyclopaedia.

- Using features of a book such as its date to determine its reliability.
- Making notes on a particular book, or passage, by jotting down the main ideas of paragraphs as they are read.
- Interpreting graphs and tables.
- Consulting several books on a subject before beginning to present the information gained.
- Presenting information in a variety of ways, including illustrated booklets, 3-D models, tape recordings etc.

Fourth year juniors
- Consolidation of first-, second- and third-year skills.

- Understanding the guide given to pronunciation in a dictionary.
- Using an adult dictionary to determine meanings and spellings of words encountered.
- Using a full range of library skills to find and review relevant material.
- Organising notes taken on a book or article into headings and sub headings.
- Synthesising information from a variety of sources.
- Presenting information in the form of a reasoned argument.

Chapter Four

Using resources

During most types of project work, children will need access to various sources of information. Some teachers collect the information first before presenting it to the children. One of the main potential benefits of project work, however, is that it gives children practice in collecting and using sources of information for themselves. If the teacher always accesses the information, this opportunity will be missed.

The range of resources

The first source of information which usually springs to mind is books. Of course, they are an extremely valuable source of information, and children should certainly learn how to use them to find the information they require. It is, however, possible to overstate their importance as an information source. Many children learn that the book is the most highly valued resource in school, and are then surprised to find that in the world outside school, most of the information they regularly need is not, in fact, contained in books.

Let's examine some common facts. We may need to know when the Battle of Waterloo took place or what the boiling point of water is. For this kind of information, a book is the most logical place to look.

However, we are far more likely to want to know things like: what is the time of the next train to London? or for how long do I cook this frozen pizza? or how do I fill in this question on my tax form? In the first resort we won't use printed materials to obtain our answers. We will, instead, ask someone else, and then, if they don't know, turn to print, whether it be a timetable, set of instructions, newspaper or computer data.

We therefore have to ensure that children become familiar with a wider range of sources of information than simply books. This range should include, perhaps above all, human resources, and children should learn the correct way of questioning other people so that they get the answers they require.

Human resources

Asking questions the right way is a skill in itself, and children will need practice in it. In a project and, indeed, in any school activity, the opportunities to ask questions of knowledgeable people will be limited unless we provide them. We can either bring people into the classroom, or take the children out to meet them.

We have already discussed the benefits of having visitors in school. Children will also have the opportunity to talk to other people when they are on a visit. For both types of meetings the children should be prepared beforehand to use the resource effectively. As well as being prepared to ask questions, the children should be ready to listen to the answers.

Asking questions

Teachers are often disappointed with the questions their children ask visitors. They may seem banal and lacking in interest and, if the children are shy, halting and poorly expressed. This is largely the result of poor preparation. For the visitor, who may be unused to talking to children, a group who are prepared will be easier to deal with and respond to

than one whose interest has to be kept alive at all costs.

Start preparing the children a few days before the visit. Explain to the children whom they will be talking to, and what kinds of interesting things they may be told. Encourage them to share their previous relevant experiences, and generally try to stimulate their interest. As this develops, ask what they would like to find out from the visitor. With younger children you may, at this stage, jot down on the chalkboard some questions which arise.

With slightly older children, you can put them into groups of four to five, and give them perhaps 20—30 minutes in which to discuss and formulate questions they may ask the visitor. Have a class feedback session, and decide on two or three questions each group could ask. A favourite question should be selected to be asked first in case there isn't time to ask all the questions.

On the day of the visit remind the class of the questions they talked about, and of what they would like to find out from the visitor. Even with older children it is best not to have them read their questions out from a prepared sheet; this appears unspontaneous and stilted. With younger children it will not work anyway. If the preparation has been done thoroughly as described, the class will remember enough interesting things to ask, and their questions will be more interesting for being more spontaneously worded.

Listening to answers

Many teachers complain at times that their children cannot or will not listen. However, listening to a different person telling them things which interest them is perhaps the best way of making the

children listen properly. They will, nevertheless, benefit from some preparatory work, although this is likely to be a long-term task.

The main points to bear in mind are that children must be interested in what is being said, and they must be capable of understanding most of it. We cannot absolutely ensure either of these, but we can help them along the way. Stimulate the children's interest before the visitor arrives by some prior discussion and work on the topic. This is also necessary to ensure that the children know enough about the topic of the visitor's talk for it to make sense.

The golden word is preparation. Remember to use the most common human resources in the classroom — the children and, especially, the teacher. Encourage children to ask and answer questions whenever they are working.

The environment

The world around us is a rich source of information, and most teachers are aware of the importance of children looking carefully at the world outside and obtaining information from it. To this end most children are at some stage taken on educational visits, usually in connection with a project.

Using the visit as a starting point for a project was discussed in an earlier chapter, but visits can, of course, be an important resource at any point during a project. There is no substitute for first-hand experience of the environment, and a great amount of knowledge can be learned by children on a visit if they are prepared beforehand.

It is a common sight to see children on a school visit armed with check-lists or worksheets which they have to complete during the visit. This can be an effective way of making them observe carefully and remember what they have seen. It will work best, however, if the visit, and the check-list have been thoroughly discussed beforehand. If the discussion is thorough enough, the children may be so enthusiastic that they do not actually need the worksheet!

If too great an emphasis is placed on completing a worksheet, or it is too long or involved, children will be distracted from carefully observing their surroundings. Here are some guidelines on preparing this kind of worksheet.

Keep it short
Even for top juniors, worksheets longer than three pages of A4 paper are probably too long. It is better to concentrate children's minds on a few subjects, which they can look at in some depth, rather than asking them to look at everything.

Aim for open-ended questions
Open-ended questions provide more scope for reaction from the children, and thus may have a longer lasting effect. Questions which ask them to note down series of facts may provide a lot of information for follow-up work in the classroom, but will probably soon be forgotten.

Include some drawing
Questions which ask children to sketch what they see can provide the opportunity to gather alternative types of information. These questions will encourage them to observe carefully, and may replace several 'one-word answer' questions. They also allow for a collection of information which cannot really be conveyed by words. Of course, children's abilities to sketch what they see will vary a great deal, not only according to their natural talents, but also in response to the previous practice and encouragement they have had in observational drawing.

Use group worksheets

Children on a visit do not all have to complete the *same* sections of a worksheet. If they are given the worksheet to complete as a group, and given time for discussion before the visit, they can allocate particular sections to individuals within the group. This spreads the burden, and also gives individual children a responsibility within their group. They may not mind an incomplete worksheet if all they risk is the teacher's displeasure, but if this lets down their friends' work, they may be more conscientious.

Children's input

There are two important factors in allowing the children to help design the worksheets. Firstly, it ensures that they are prepared for what they are likely to see on the visit. Secondly, they have had some say in deciding the work to be done during the visit, and may consequently be more committed to it.

Information books

While books will not be the only source of information during project work, they remain very important. Children will need access to as wide a range of information books as possible, and they will need to be taught how to use them.

Selecting information books

Financial constraints make it unlikely that teachers will ever have available all the books they would like. They have to select from the many books published and make appropriate choices for the children they are dealing with. You should look for certain criteria in information books, although circumstances might dictate that you have to make the best of what is offered.

Clearly children will be drawn more to attractively presented books. The cover, the size of typeface, the amount of colour and the general appearance are all likely to attract children and make them *want* to use it as a source of information. These features are not absolutely vital, however, and several books might be lacking in these but compensate by being good in other ways.

The arrangement of the book is perhaps the key criterion for a good children's information book. It should be possible to find information within the book in a systematic way. This means that features such as a list of contents and an index are essential. Without them, children are forced to search by browsing, which most teachers try to discourage in information-seeking activities.

Information books are often designed to have different aims. Some are almost story-books with the information hidden within them. Others are designed around colour spread pictures, and the information contained in the text is of secondary importance. Others are organised on the lines of an encyclopaedia with information presented in carefully arranged chunks. Each of these has its attractions, and all are useful to project work. Each, however, demands a very different approach from the child reader, and children should know how to use each type effectively.

A final point to look for is the book's general perspective. Despite the fact that for many years we have lived in a multicultural society, there has been a tendency for children's information books either to ignore ethnic minority groups, or to portray them in a patronising way. There are now many more books which present information from the perspectives of various ethnic minorities. All children should become aware, through the books they use, of alternative viewpoints on the world.

Teaching the use of books
Children should be taught how to use reference books from the first time they handle them. Specific techniques, like using the index or the contents page, can be discussed with young children. They should begin to use these techniques naturally, just as they learned, for example, which way up a book should be, or where you begin reading a page. The more they become familiar with these techniques in the early years, the less direct teaching they will need later on.

Perhaps most importantly, the teacher should not forget the importance of her own behaviour in the classroom. She needs to *demonstrate* effective ways of finding information, as well as telling children how it is done.

More suggestions for practice in using information books are given in the Appendix, together with a list of sources of further exercises (see page 123). Guidelines for using exercises of this kind are given in the next chapter.

Fiction
Story-books are an often neglected source of information for project work. Literature can give a fresh perspective to most projects, not only to the obvious historical and geographical projects. It can also be used as a starting point for project work.

The topic webs given on pages 72 and 73 show how projects might be developed using *Stig of the Dump* and *Little Grey Rabbit's Birthday* as starting points.

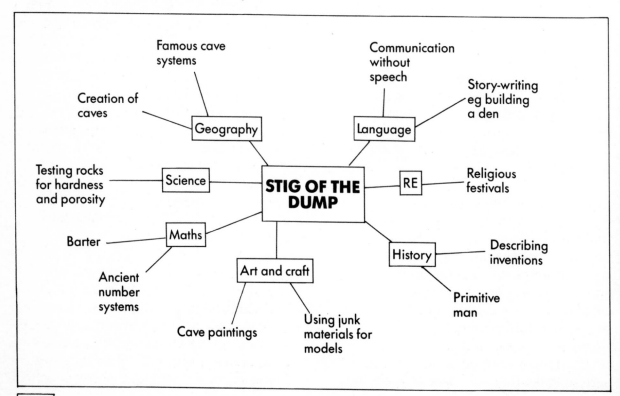

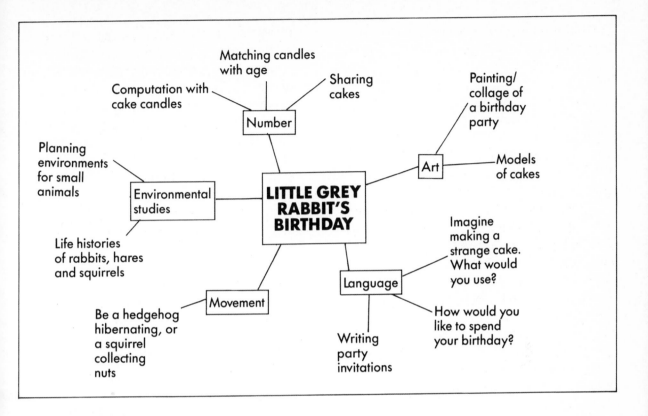

When you use a story in project work, there are two important points to bear in mind. Firstly, a story has its own reason for being, and is not simply a support for project work. Work using stories should always be true to their themes. For example, *The Wheel on the School* is set in Holland but this does not mean that it is best used as a starting point for work on Holland. The book is not *about* Holland, but rather about problems and human relationships; work using the book should centre around these themes.

Secondly, using a story as a starting point for a project should not mean a return to the 'set-book' approach familiar in secondary school literature teaching. Too much emphasis on 'studying' the book, with worksheets, comprehension passages etc, is likely to result only in a lessening of children's enjoyment, and so become self-defeating.

Other resources
The vast range of information sources other than books which children need to be familiar with includes the following:

- magazines,
- brochures,
- advertisements,
- pamphlets,
- forms,
- timetables,
- instructions,
- maps,
- computer databases,
- slide sets,
- cassette recordings,
- video recordings,
- posters.

Here are suggestions on how to use them in project work.

Magazines

Most children will be familiar with magazines at home, and children will be able to bring into school those useful for their particular project. Even if the information they contain is not much use, they often provide a good source of pictures. These can be cut up, mounted on card and stored so that everyone can consult them when needed. By their nature they tend to be up-to-date, which is sometimes more than can be said for many of the books in school libraries!

Their drawback is that they are not usually systematically arranged as information books are, and may contain a wide variety of articles, some of which will be of little use, while others are useful in several projects. This problem can be alleviated by cutting up the magazine into separate sections and storing each article in a separate document wallet. These can be added to as more articles are collected and can form a useful resource. Many teachers already do this with teachers' magazines such as *Child Education* and *Junior Education.*

Brochures

Brochures are usually forms of advertising but, as long as the observations under the next heading are noted, they can be a useful resource. Holiday brochures are popular sources of information on countries, sporting activities, forms of transport as well as holidays. They can also give children practice in filling in forms and in number work as they work out the cost of particular holidays. Their final advantage is, of course, that they are free!

Advertisements

Advertisements can provide useful information but they also allow children to develop a critical approach to information handling. Because the information they present is designed to persuade, advertisements tend to be approached by most adults with some scepticism (even though they may in the end be persuasive). Children tend to be more susceptible to advertisements, and it is worth pointing out to children the techniques used by advertisers. If children become more sceptical of advertisements, this attitude may rub off on to other sources of information.

Children, like many adults, seem to believe implicitly that print is infallible; anything that shakes this belief is useful. Project work may give children the opportunity to design their own advertisements. This will also give them insights into the techniques used by the advertiser.

Pamphlets

Many pamphlets provide information in an easily accessible form. They include pamphlets issued by British Coal on mining in Britain, by the World Wildlife Fund on conservation and those available at post offices on aspects of the postal service. Most of these are free, and can be obtained by the children. They are easy to store, up-to-date, readily available and thus expendable.

Forms

While not actually being a source of information, forms can be filled in by children during a project to give them useful practical experience. Some projects will have little place for this kind of activity, but in others it can be a major feature. In a project on holidays, for example, third year juniors filled in holiday booking forms, passport application forms and questionnaires about their holidays.

Timetables

Many adults have difficulty using timetables. Most primary mathematics schemes include work on their use, but project work provides the opportunity for children to use *real* timetables rather than invented ones. They are most effective if the children have a real information problem whose solution depends on reading the timetable accurately.

For example, one group of children had to organise their class trip to the sea-shore. They had to consult the local bus timetable to plan departure and arrival times. As they did this they were also given several other exercises to increase their familiarity with the timetable. They were happy to do this as they could see a clear purpose in it.

A project on flight included much work on airline timetables. This was brought closer to reality when the class visited an airport and pretended to catch a particular plane. In a project on 'our town', children co-ordinated bus and rail timetables to check the places within one hour's travelling time.

Instructions

Reading and acting upon instructions can be a regular activity in the classroom, and can fit in with many projects. It is a feature of adult life as we follow a recipe, use a new electrical appliance, assemble a piece of kit furniture etc. Children can do similar activities in project work, such as conducting an experiment on woodlice in a project on mini-beasts, or making

paper aeroplanes in a flight project. Projects can also encourage children to write instructions for others to follow.

Maps

The interpretation and construction of maps can be a part of many projects. When looking at railways, children can trace old railway lines on a map of the local area, and then try to find them on the ground. In work on the Romans, the Vikings, or the Normans, children can find settlements, plot voyages and conquests, and look for the evidence of place names on maps.

Computer databases

The computer is a relatively new resource in the classroom, but as a source of information it is potentially the most powerful of all. Database programs store vast amounts of information and children need to learn new skills to retrieve and use this information.

Many children will already be familiar with a teletext service: that is, a nationally available computer database which is provided by the major television companies. The service contains vast amounts of regularly updated information, much of which can be useful in project work.

With an even greater potential use is the telephone viewdata system, Prestel, although this does not as yet have the same number of home users. As well as containing a much larger and more varied collection of information, Prestel also has the advantage of being interactive. Users can send as well as receive information and messages via the telephone system. This type of electronic mail service is gradually being introduced into schools and those who use it in project work have an enormous advantage over those who don't.

The types of information held by electronic mail services include news headlines, weather forecasts, information on products from cars to computers, tourist information about countries and resorts, train and airline timetables and fares, sports fixtures and results, popular music charts, facts and figures on almost any subject, and details of where to send for specialised information on most subjects.

On a smaller scale, several software packages allow children to store and manipulate their own information about any subject which interests them. The speed and power of the computer makes it possible to collate and extract data far quicker than by sorting through books and other written sources of information. To illustrate some of the potential of a database, here is part of a first year junior project on dinosaurs.

The children decided that some of their work would require them to collect information about a range of different dinosaurs. They discussed the kind of information they would need and arrived at a list of headings:

Name ....
Length ....
Height ....
Weight ....
Meat or plant eater ....
Habitat ....
Size of footprint ....
Special features ....

A database was prepared using these headings as field names. The children collected information on 21 different types of dinosaur, and entered it into the database.

The data was sorted several times according to various headings such as the height of dinosaurs in ascending order, or their length. These lists were then printed out. The program was used to draw pie charts of dinosaur diets and their habitats and to draw histograms of length, weight, diet etc. It also drew graphs of, for example, weight against footprint size, and these were used to discuss relationships between data. The children decided that, in general, the heavier the dinosaur, the bigger its footprint, but there was no link between weight and whether the dinosaur ate plants or meat. The printed graphs, along with the children's comments, were used as part of the project's display work.

Most of the children in the class had a turn at questioning the data, such as, 'What was the heaviest meat eater?' or 'Was there a link between where dinosaurs lived and their size?' They also discussed at length the possible explanations for the answers given. All these activities could have been done without the aid of the computer, but much more laboriously and slowly.

Slide sets
A great deal of information can be conveyed by pictures, and slides represent one of the most convenient ways of storing large numbers of them. Many schools have slide collections, which are usually organised on a topic basis. These are usually used by the teacher when looking for suitable slides to show the class for their project work. Some slides can be stored in the classroom where they can be consulted by individual children.

For his class who were doing a project on railways, one teacher collected several slides from a set on 'Transport on land',

and added several he had taken himself at a railway museum. These were given to a group of children who numbered them, and listed what each one showed. The teacher obtained several individual small plastic wallets into which each of the slides was placed and then glued to a 15cm by 10cm catalogue card. The number of the slide and details of its contents were written on the card. On the back of each card were written three questions about the slide, which required children either to look very closely at it, or to do some research elsewhere. The completed slide set was stored in a catalogue card box and kept near a portable slide viewer. The set was then used both as a source of information, and as a stimulus for children who needed guidance on what to do in their projects.

Cassette- and video-recordings
As with slide sets, it is more usual for teachers to build up and use personal or school libraries of audio- and video-

cassettes, than it is for children to consult them. Such useful sources of information can, however, be effectively used by individuals and groups of children. The cassettes need to be kept in order, and catalogued with full descriptions of their contents.

With audio-cassettes it is best to record one item on one cassette. Short play cassettes are very useful. C60s are easily available, while C30s and C15s which are intended for use as computer tapes are perfectly acceptable and fairly cheap. For video-cassettes, a full catalogue description with reference numbers are necessary to avoid children having to play through unwanted material to find the item they require.

The cassettes need to be stored within easy range of playback facilities, and teachers must ensure that children can operate the machinery sensibly. Keep clearly written instructions close to the machines or delegate a few children as 'consultants' to help those who have problems.

Posters
Posters are an attractive source of information, and can often be obtained at very little cost from such organisations as British Telecom or the Milk Marketing Board. *Child Education* and *Junior Education* are also excellent sources of display material. Centralised storage is probably more suitable for items like this, with each class in a school having a full descriptive catalogue of the collection. This will allow children to check whether the collection has any useful material for their work, without having to browse through it. As with all collections of information, it is better to encourage children to look for specific items, rather than having vague ideas in mind.

Storage and access

The widest ranging and most comprehensive collection of resources is of little use unless it can be stored so that it is easily accessible by teachers and especially by children. Each type of resource has its own storage problems to which there will be many solutions depending on the circumstances of the school.

Most schools will have a centralised store of resources, ranging from a central library area to a collection of slides and posters in the staffroom. This is a good idea where resources are scarce, as it means everyone has access to them. It can, however, have drawbacks.

• If the resources are stored for the teachers' benefit, say in the staffroom, children often don't have the opportunity to learn how to access them.

• A large collection of resources, while useful in terms of choice, may actually be confusing for young children.

• Access to a central collection may have to be limited because of heavy demand, which may mean lost opportunities for teaching the skills of accessing the resources.

Because of such problems, it is usual for some resources to be kept in classrooms in addition to the central store. These are not as wide-ranging, but are immediately accessible. Younger children can be taught important reference skills in the familiar surroundings of their own classroom, using manageable collections, before being expected to handle the full school resource collection. There is, therefore, a

need for both central and classroom-based resource collections. Deciding on where particular resources should be stored will depend upon particular circumstances.

The storage system used for any resource collection needs to be clear and easy to understand. The main point of having a system is that children should be able to locate the items they need by using deliberate, efficient strategies. If the system is too complex for them to understand, they will resort to browsing and finding resources by accident. The storage system should be designed with the children in mind, rather than just being convenient for adults. Systems such as the Simplified Dewey System are specifically designed for use with younger children.

The storage system should be standard throughout a school, and children systematically introduced to it. This avoids confusion, and lets the school develop a coherent policy for teaching information skills.

Usually there is no problem regarding a central collection, as most schools only have one, but problems may occur in ensuring that classroom resource collections are organised according to the school system. This is important for the sake of continuity, even if the collection only has a few items. With only 15 books, two pamphlets and ten slides, it may seem unnecessary to organise them according to the Dewey System. Children can, after all, see at a glance exactly what is there. This miniature system will, however, allow children to become familiar with the storage system in a manageable and secure situation.

Standardisation does not imply that there can be no development in the storage system throughout a school.

Older children can be introduced to more sophisticated methods, as long as the basic system remains the same. For example, some schools use almost a complete Dewey System in their top junior classes, the Simplified Dewey System for the lower juniors, and a colour-based version of Dewey with the top infants. Each school should decide on a systematic policy which will work for them.

Children should be consulted about the storage of resources and their access. They should also be asked for their suggestions for improving the system.

As an example, a class of second year juniors were asked to organise the resources for their project on the Egyptians. When sorting out their reference books, they suggested that it would save time if they made comments

79

about each book on a catalogue card. They would then be able to pick out quickly books which met their particular requirements. With some help from the teacher, they devised a colour system, as follows:

A blue dot meant the book was very easy.
A red dot meant it was difficult to read.
A green dot meant it was average.
A yellow dot meant it had very good pictures.

After using this system for a while some of them asked to extend it to include:
A brown dot for books which had a wider interest than just the Egyptians, eg ancient history.
A black dot for books on narrower subjects, eg the pyramids.

Children can also take part in choosing which resources they should have, and in obtaining them. This can be discussed in the planning stage of the project. Some schools encourage children to visit the local bookshop, sometimes with the teacher, to choose books. One school allocated a certain sum of money for each class to purchase books, although this had to include fiction as well as information books. By arrangement with the local bookseller, each teacher took his or her class into the shop, where they chose one book each for the school. When the books arrived at school, each was labelled inside with the name of the child who chose it. The children were naturally very proud of 'their' books, and recommended them to everyone.

Other resources can be collected by children from shops, post offices, travel agents, libraries, museums, tourist information offices etc. With parents' help this can become a whole family activity.

Developing skills to use resources

Some children will easily pick up the necessary skills to use resources well, but the majority require a systematic teaching programme. This is more effective if it is planned on a school basis rather than being a haphazard collection of the efforts of individual teachers.

It is better to teach skills in meaningful contexts than to teach them as a separate activity. If children are taught skills when they need them, they are more likely to learn and retain them. If, however, the skills are taught in separate lessons, children are likely to have problems in transferring them to other situations. This is not to say that there is no place for 'study skills exercises', which many educational publishing firms now produce, but that the methods of using these materials should be considered carefully. Integrating them into project work will make them a more purposeful activity for children.

The following example will help to illustrate this approach. In a class of third year juniors, one group of children was collecting the answers to a series of questions they had devised about several popular holiday destinations. The teacher noticed that they tended to look for information in books by leafing through the pages. He showed them how to use the index pages and followed this up by suggesting that they complete an exercise from one of their workbooks on the use of the index. The children were able to understand why they were doing the exercise, and could see that it would help them complete their own tasks more effectively.

Children will not learn to use resources unless they have opportunities and the need to do so. Make sure, therefore, that children need to use a whole range of resources on a regular basis. Records should be kept of the type of resources that children have used and how they have used them.

Making mistakes in handling resources can have positive results. Teachers occasionally have difficulty in standing back from children as they are working, allowing them to make mistakes and then realising the consequences. If children's mistakes are pointed out straight away, they do not get the chance to realise for themselves what went wrong. To improve next time around they must remember what they were told. This is less efficient than finding out for themselves.

It is not usually sufficient to tell children how to use particular resources. More often they need to be *shown* how to do it. More effective still is showing them and explaining exactly what you are doing and why. The children should then be left to try for themselves.

People who use resources effectively are able to tell when they did a particular task well and when they could have done it better. Children can begin to develop these abilities at quite an early stage if they are encouraged to think about how well they performed certain tasks. Ask children regularly about what they did, how they found particular pieces of information, and whether they think they could do it any better. This can be done on an individual basis, but is also especially effective with small groups. Make this kind of question occur naturally as the children work by themselves, so that they become more aware of their own performance and can correct it if necessary.

Chapter Five

The project underway

In an earlier chapter I suggested that children should begin a project with a clear idea of what they are trying to achieve. They should therefore know the type of end products they are aiming for, whether these are booklets, wallcharts or whatever, and for whom they are being produced. These goals should not be inflexible. As the project progresses, new ideas may emerge and you may have to change or expand your original plans.

Working towards a product

From the teacher's point of view, the end product of a project is, in a way, of small importance. The learning process through which children go during project work is far more important. Two examples, which many teachers will recognise, will make this clear.

In the first example, a group of children produce a beautifully presented booklet on ships. It has a contents page which shows that each page is concerned with a different type of ship. On each page there is a cut-out colour illustration of a ship and underneath two or three paragraphs of very neat writing about it. On closer inspection, it is obvious that almost all the writing has been painstakingly copied from reference books.

In the second example, a group produce a somewhat scruffy wallchart on aeroplanes. In the centre is a hand-drawn picture of a jumbo jet, with labels

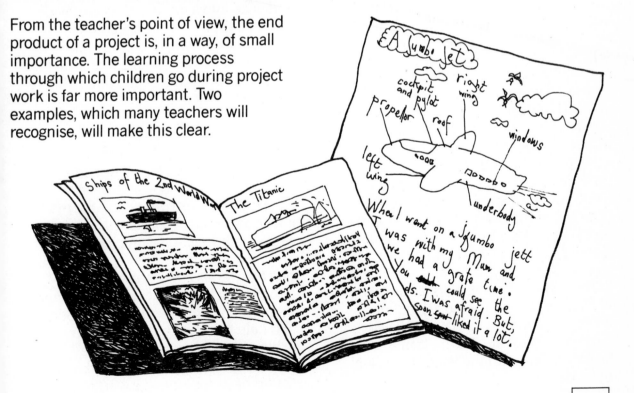

describing the various parts. Under this is an account of one child's journey in a jumbo jet. Around the wallchart are various sketches of other types of aeroplanes, accompanied by pieces of writing ranging from poems to imaginary accounts of flying. All the writing has spelling mistakes and crossings out, and some of it is quite difficult to read.

I chose these two examples deliberately because it is likely that both groups had a similar outcome in mind when they began their work. The first group seems to have paid more attention to the presentation of their work, but what they have learned in the process is probably very little. The second group needs some assistance with the presentation of their work, but they have undoubtedly learned far more, both in looking carefully at pictures, and in trying to link the information they have found to their own experiences.

The end product remains important, however, for two clear reasons. Firstly, as adults we are often judged according to what we produce. The end product of any task is often the only visible result of our efforts. Children need to learn how to make what they produce satisfactory for the situation and appropriate for the people who will receive it.

Secondly, the end product is usually the children's main goal in a project. Most children are disheartened if this does not reach a certain standard, and no amount of reassurance that they have learned a lot in the process will compensate.

The ways in which children's project work is usually presented are rather limited and later in this chapter I will suggest a range of different formats, but first I will deal with the important issue of audience.

Aiming for an audience

When we try to communicate ideas, whether through writing or other media, we usually have a fairly clear idea of our audience. They can affect the format and the content of our communication to a large extent. If, for example, I am involved in a car crash, I may write about the events to my insurance company, and also to my best friend. The basic information will be the same in both cases, but the particular details I include and, more noticeably, the style in which I write will be very different. It would not be appropriate to write in the same way to both audiences.

Most of us are aware of this and act accordingly. With less experience, children need to be taught to take their audience into account. We can provide a range of audiences for children to communicate with, and project work is well suited to this. The children's main audiences are the teacher, other children and other adults.

The teacher
In most cases, even if project work is ultimately destined for other audiences, the first people to look at it will be teachers. They are, therefore, the most important audience for children's project work. Their reactions are crucial.

The teacher as a trusted adult
Usually teachers want children to trust them to view their work sympathetically and help them with it. Those who achieve this are in very privileged positions. Not only is mutual trust a sound basis for effective learning and

teaching, but it can also provide specific opportunities for children to develop in their writing abilities in particular. One of the best ways for children to learn about writing is for them to experiment, to try out new words and new expressions. To encourage them to do this, teachers must be sure that they respond positively to such experiments. To respond with criticism or by marking experiments as mistakes, will only destroy children's trust and will discourage them from experimenting in future.

The teacher as an examiner
Teachers often receive children's work in the role of examiners. They 'mark' children's work and they 'correct' mistakes. This can, rather too often, discourage children rather than encourage them. This is the negative side of being regarded as an examiner by the children.

There can be, however, a more positive side to the teacher's examiner role. When producing work which they think is important, most children are keen that the work is presentable and correct. Children will take pride in their work when given the opportunity and encouraged to produce their best. Teachers are invaluable in this process as they have more experience to judge children's work than the children have. Children can use their teachers as preliminary testers of their work before passing it on to its intended audience.

This use of the teacher-as-examiner role is very child-centred, since the children have to recognise that teachers are best equipped to comment on their work. It is a positive sign indeed if children approach teachers with their work asking for it to be corrected. They have both recognised the need to present their work in its best light, and also decided that the teacher is the best person to do this properly.

The teacher in a special role
By putting themselves in roles special to a particular piece of work, teachers can provide a third kind of audience for children's project work.

In one project, top juniors planned how best to use a piece of waste ground near the school. One group pretended they were property developers, and put forward their plans accordingly. A second group pretended to be local farmers, and a third an environmental pressure group. Part of the project involved writing letters arguing their case to people such as local councillors and residents. These letters were sent to the teacher, who replied to each in the correct role.

In another project, first year juniors designed new homes for the Iron Man. Their designs were sent to the teacher, who replied to each, pretending to be the Iron Man, with an assessment of how appropriate the design would be for him.

In a third project, on magic, top infants wrote magic spells and sent them to a witch to test out. The witch (teacher) wrote back to each child with an account of what happened when she tried the spells. This became a longer running project than the teacher had anticipated, as some children wrote back to the witch with suggested improvements to their spells. They eventually picked out the best spells and sent them to the witch in a presentation volume.

In all of these examples the children knew that they were writing to their teacher. They were able to suspend disbelief because of the teachers' abilities to carry off their roles successfully.

Other children

After the teacher, the most usual audience for children's project work is other children, whether they are in the same class, the same school or attend another school.

Children in the same class

Most children have their work read by their classmates at some time during their school career. Pieces of work are displayed so that other children can look at them and read them. In these cases the audience is almost an incidental part of the work. To develop children's sensitivity to the needs of various audiences, children need to produce work with, for example, their classmates in mind. There are several ways of doing this.

Children can be given time to 'present' their work to the rest of the class. This is most likely to happen as children complete their work on particular projects, but it can be done at regular intervals throughout a project and, as we will see later, it can be a useful evaluation technique. When children know that they will present their project work to their classmates, they have to tailor their presentation to that particular audience. They need to bear their audience in mind as they work on their project, and can be given advice on presentation, etc, by the teacher as necessary.

If the project is intended to result in a class-based presentation of work, such as a class book, magazine, or central display, a group of children can be given the role of 'editorial board'. All work produced will initially go to this board, possibly via the teacher. The board has to advise on its suitability, perhaps suggest changes, select suitable pieces and plan the final product.

Class-based project work thus has two audiences: those who will see the final product, and the editorial board which has to approve material for this final product. A scheme like this will emphasise the appreciation of audience for all the children, but especially for those children on the editorial board. They have to judge the appropriateness

of the work for the intended audience, justify to others why particular pieces are not appropriate as they stand, and give useful guidance on how work might be better presented. Membership of this board should be varied so that most children have the chance to participate.

Children's project work can be presented in a format which can be stored permanently in the classroom library, and read and used by their classmates. This is a particularly valuable exercise. Not only does it encourage children to consider their audience, but it also gives their work a high status. Project booklets which are to be stored will probably need to be bound in hard covers and made from good quality paper if they are to survive any length of time. This is a useful activity in its own right.

Children in other classes
There are two common ways of presenting children's project work to children in other classes. The project can be displayed in part of the school used by other classes, such as the corridor or the assembly hall. Alternatively, the class can present a school assembly based on their project. The latter is a particularly useful activity, as children have to tailor their material to a wide range of ages and abilities. Both these methods are, however, limited in their effects on children's audience awareness because of the lack of real feedback. Children will only learn about the needs of an audience if they have the opportunity to hear the responses of that audience to their work.

One way of providing this feedback is for classes to team up to work on linked projects, at the end of which their

presentations can be swapped. In one example of this, a class of third year juniors and another class of mixed second and third years decided to do a project together on the development of land transport, focusing especially on their home county. One class decided to specialise in transport by railway and the other in road transport. The classes were occasionally brought together to see slides and films about transport. As the classes swapped completed pieces of work, both found that information about topics related to their own gave them fresh insights into their areas and caused them to rethink their work. It is only fair to say that co-operation like this is only successful when the two classes are of roughly equal maturity and ability.

Older classes can produce project work for younger classes. This clearly benefits the older children as it gives their work a real purpose and audience, but it can also benefit the younger ones since it gives them 'information books' which are specifically designed for them. One class of second year juniors did a project on animals, in which they had to prepare booklets on wild animals for a top infant class. They began by borrowing examples of the information books that were already in the infant class to study and assess the format and style in which they were written. This was, in fact, not very successul and it would have been better had the junior children, or at least some of them, visited the infants and talked to them about the kind of books they used.

The children then started their project and decided that they would produce 12 short booklets, each dealing with one animal, such as tiger, lion etc. They discussed the format of the books, and decided that they needed lots of pictures and only short pieces of writing. Each of the six project groups in the class took responsibility for two booklets. When the books were finished, but not yet bound, one representative from each group took their books to the infant class and let some of the children read them and talk about them. As a result of this 'consumer research' they were able to suggest changes to the booklets. These were then implemented, and the books bound in hard covers before they were presented to the infants and put into their class library.

As well as producing project books for class libraries, children can also contribute to the school library. Books can be stored as a special collection, or integrated into the rest of the library, with their own Dewey numbers etc.

Children in other schools
Producing project work for children in other schools can be a very useful way of providing a real purpose for the

presentation of this work, as well as giving opportunities for developing an awareness of audience. Two ways in which this can be done are described below.

One class of third year juniors developed a long relationship with a similar class in a different part of the country. (Their teachers had been friends at college.) The two classes were paired one for one, and regularly kept in touch with each other as pen-friends. They also exchanged project work. At the beginning of the year each class began with a similar project on their local environment. The main purpose was to tell their friends all about where they lived. As one school was situated in a rural area in the north of England and the other in a London suburb, there were many differences to learn about. The classes exchanged project booklets, photographs and cassette-tapes, and each mounted a display in their classroom about the other's area.

In another example, two classes of first year juniors from different parts of a large city each began the school year with a project on 'ourselves'. Copies of completed work were swapped and used in displays by the receiving classes. Cassettes and videos were also exchanged, and the project worked towards a joint party at which the classes could meet each other.

Other possibilities for this kind of work include corresponding with children in other countries. Often a town-twinning association will be able to help arrange this.

Other adults
Producing work for adults besides the teacher is possible for most schools, and can have a great impact in making

children's project work come alive. There are several possibilities.

Parents
Parents are the obvious audience to consider first. Many parents only look at their children's work on parents' consultation evenings, and on these occasions the work was not prepared especially for them, so there was no audience awareness involved. They can, though, be targetted as the chief audience for pieces of project work, and copies can be given to them when completed. Projects about the school, the local environment, or the children themselves are perhaps most appropriate.

Parents visiting school can become an extra audience. They need to be carefully guided on how to respond to children's work, but there is no reason why visiting parents cannot fulfil any of the audience roles played by the teacher, as described earlier.

Visitors and other helpers
If a project has included a visitor, the children can produce work especially for him or her. Most people who visit schools to talk to the children would be only too pleased to receive work connected with their visit.

The same applies to other people who may have assisted with the project. For example, the local chief postmaster may have replied to children's questions, as might the local stationmaster etc. Local people, such as the manager of the supermarket or the community policeman, may have been interviewed by children. Sending these people copies of work in which they played a part not only gives children practice in preparing material for a real audience, but also does much to encourage these people to help other children and schools in the future.

Local newspapers

Local newspapers are often pleased to feature work done by schools. Usually they will report on the work rather than print it as the children have produced it, but the quality of production will determine whether or not the newspaper writes about it.

Presentation

There are many possible ways in which children can present project work. Some of these ways are described below.

Booklets

Perhaps the most popular form of presentation is the project booklet. Each child usually has his own small booklet in which work on the project is recorded. Sometimes these booklets are ready-made exercise books; others are home-made books of folded paper inside a sugar-paper or card cover. Making the books can be a valuable part of the project. When finished, the books will contain a mixture of writing and drawings.

Booklets like these do have their limitations. If a piece of work does not fit into the booklet format then it doesn't count. They also enforce a linear approach to the work. It is very difficult for children to go back to work in the front part of the booklet and revise or add to it; there will probably not be space.

Loose-leaf folders

Folders which allow pages to be removed and new ones inserted are much more flexible than pre-bound booklets. They enable children to go back to a piece of work they did some time ago and revise and perhaps rewrite it. They also allow the work to be rearranged into a different order.

Being able to remove pages from these folders makes it possible to collate the work of several children on a particular aspect of the project and make a class booklet for display. Pieces of work can also be removed and displayed individually.

The ideal folder has metal rings which click open and shut but these can be expensive. A cheaper method is to tie work together with wool or string. These are, however, never satisfactory. Some children always get the string irretrievably knotted, causing great frustration for the teacher.

Posters and wallcharts

Presenting project work on wallcharts has some advantages over booklet presentation. Artwork and written work can be easily linked together and cross-referenced. Artwork which would be too bulky to fit into a booklet can be more easily included on a wallchart.

You can design a wallchart in several ways. One design is a simple version of the topic web that was used to plan the project. Collect work around each of the subtopic parts of the web. For example, a wallchart on animals might have the main title in the centre of a large frieze. Each corner could have a subtitle, such as farm animals, pets, wild animals and working animals, with related paintings, drawings, writing and charts displayed around each.

Another design is built around a large frieze/collage. A wallchart about airports might include a large frieze of an airport, with a plane on the runway, the airport buildings, and some of the workers. Beside each feature could be an accompanying piece of writing, which can either be on the chart itself, or around the edge and linked to the feature by a piece of wool or string.

Other wallchart designs might be more specific. For example, a chart on dinosaurs could have pictures of eight types of dinosaur drawn to scale, one beneath the other. Alongside each could be some facts and figures about that particular animal. Alternatively the chart might be based on a time line, with periods of a hundred million years, each accompanied by pictures and information about the dinosaurs common at that time.

Particular designs are obviously determined by the subject matter but, in general, there is a great deal to be gained if children are involved in the design of a wallchart. There may be possibilities that the teacher has not seen and they will certainly learn a great deal from working out measurements, etc, for the wallchart.

Models
A 3-D model as an end product should not be regarded simply as an opportunity for the children to practise manual skills. Making a model can require the children to put to use a great deal of information collected during the course of the project.

For example, as part of a project on railways, a group of third year juniors made models of railway engines at four points in their history. For some of their work they used pictures they had found in books, but they also had to read about these engines to ensure they had the correct details. The finished models were an excellent demonstration of their reading comprehension.

In another project, some fourth year juniors made a model of their school buildings. This entailed a great deal of measurement, consulting plans and rough sketching.

In both these examples, children had to absorb and understand information from a variety of sources before putting it to use to construct their model. This requires a higher level of understanding than when children have only to write down certain pieces of information.

Fiction
An often neglected way of presenting information is to use it as the basis for a piece of narrative. This can be especially useful in historical projects, where dry historical facts can come alive if used as the background for a story.

As an example of this, one group of second year juniors aimed, as part of their project on the Vikings, to tell the story of a Viking voyage. Before they could do this sensibly, they needed to collect information about the design of Viking ships, where the Vikings sailed to, why they made long voyages, how they organised themselves, the kinds of preparations they would make and what problems there might be.

These points were used as the basis for their information search in books and encyclopaedias. They gathered their information under each heading and used the results to plan their story. This was written collaboratively, with each child taking responsibility for a section. The whole group then commented on it and suggested changes. The result was an excellent piece of narrative writing, with a very authentic background.

Pamphlets

I shall term a pamphlet as a very short booklet, say four to six pages, dealing with one specific topic within a project. In any one project, children might produce several pamphlets. For example, in a project on communications, second year juniors produced pamphlets on the telephone, television, radio, the postal service and computers.

Having to produce short, snappy pamphlets makes children condense the information they accumulate and pick out the essential items only. This is an excellent way of getting children to consider the value of each word they use as they are writing. It is a good idea to show children at the start of a project some of the many pamphlets produced by organisations such as the Post Office.

Tape-recordings

The products of project work do not, of course, have to be in a written form. There are many advantages in children producing audio-tapes about their project. They still have to think carefully about the way they present information. A simple account of what they have found out will produce a rather dull and uninspiring presentation. Alternative ways of presenting the information have to be discussed. Presenting accounts of their work through stories or poems may be more exciting. Mock interviews, or documentary-style presentations may also be more engaging for the listener.

Children might also consider tape-slide presentations, with their audio-tapes linked to a series of slides or pictures. To add extra interest, they could use a magazine-type approach. One of the main benefits of this form of presentation is that it does not discriminate against children with poor handwriting.

Video-recordings

Most of the advantages of sound recordings apply also to video-recordings, although these have extra potential by allowing pictures and sound to be closely linked. Those children fortunate enough to have access to a video-recorder and camera can learn a whole range of new skills, and will be encouraged to pay great attention to the presentation of their project work and its impact. If you do not have your own video equipment, you may find that your local secondary school, or college of further or higher education may loan items, or offer to show children how to use the equipment.

Diagrams

Often it is more appropriate for children to present information in diagrammatic form than in written prose. This has the advantage of making sure children really understand the information they present and making it impossible for them to copy from information books.

There are many types of diagram which they may use, depending on the type of information they have. A matrix is often useful. The example below is the result of a project on animals in which second and third year juniors discovered how animals might be classified.

Other types of diagram include graphs (a block graph to show in which countries children have spent holidays), maps (a map showing the growth of railway lines in Britain), and flow charts (a flow chart showing the sequence of events in the production of electricity).

With a wide range of formats available for presenting information discovered during project work, and with a variety of audiences to bear in mind, there is little excuse for allowing children to copy chunks of text from reference books. Coping with the demands of presentation is a powerful learning experience in its own right.

Characteristic	Type of animal				
	Mammal	Reptile	Insect	Bird	Fish
Warm-blooded	✔	✕	✕	✔	✕
Lays eggs	◯	✔	✔	✔	✔
Has lungs	✔	✔	✕	✔	◯
Flies	◯	✕	◯	✔	✕
Suckles young	✔	✕	✕	✕	✕
Has skin	✔	✕	✕	✔	✕
Has scales	✕	✔	✕	✕	✔
Lives in water	◯	◯	◯	✕	✔

Key: ✔ Yes ✕ No ◯ Sometimes

Quizzes

Designing quizzes for other members of the class based on a project area can be a real stimulus for children to accumulate information. Before they can ask sensible questions in a quiz, children need not only to know the answers themselves, but also to have a sufficiently broad understanding of the subject to know what the important questions are.

Quizzes can be set as general knowledge activities, with the class counting their scores of correct answers, or you may like to devise more complicated competitions. Each group taking part in the project could set a number of questions on the area they have been studying. The questions could be displayed in the classroom and the whole class then has two or three days to find as many answers as they can, either working individually or in their groups. Another competition might run along the lines of *Trivial Pursuit* with each group responsible for a question area.

Chapter Six

The teacher's role

The teacher has many roles to play during project work, some of which will be described here. It is essential to remember that project work is a time for learning and for teaching, so the teacher's role should involve a great deal more than sitting back, allowing children to 'get on with it'. There is certainly a temptation for teachers to think that, having prepared the ground, helped children sort out their aims, and planned exactly how they will go about it, the children's motivation will be enough to keep them working.

Many teachers will testify that a classful of children working enthusiastically on their project seems to need little attention from the teacher, who is free to do other tasks like hear individual children read, or withdraw groups for extra tuition in basic skills. However, if this is the teacher's role in project work, then a great deal of potential is being lost. Because children are highly motivated to complete work, this provides the best opportunity to teach them many skills. The teacher should, therefore, have a clear teaching role during project work.

The teacher's role may keep him or her from intervening in children's work at times. All learners, adults and children alike, learn best when they see the need to learn. Children working on a project which interests them will often find that there are tasks they want to do but do not know how. In the right kind of environment, they should be able to ask for their teacher's guidance. Their learning ought to be more effective as they have identified their needs. If this is to happen, the teacher will be acting as consultant, rather than director of children's work. He or she will need to stand back and allow children to decide for themselves when to ask for advice. This can, of course, be a difficult role to play, as it may mean watching children make mistakes but not interfering until the mistakes become apparent to the children themselves.

The teacher should, however, structure occasions when children ask for advice. As the project is planned, the teacher could suggest activities which are likely to encourage children to ask for help. This will involve the type of negotiation we have previously considered.

The teacher's role in project work will therefore be as consultant, poser of problems, facilitator and helper, as well as being, of course, teacher.

Teaching during the project

Many times during the project, teachers will wish to teach the children, rather than simply allow them to learn by doing. They may, for example, want to teach certain facts, or particular skills. We must look closely at the organisation of this teaching and its nature.

Organisation
When teachers feel that some direct teaching is required, they must consider whether this should be on an individual, group or class basis. Sometimes it is better to treat the class as a whole and take class lessons on particular topics. At other times it is preferable to teach one group at a time. Not all class members will require this teaching, and it can be

directed at certain groups. Finally, it may sometimes be appropriate to teach individuals.

In a project on holidays with third year juniors, the class was put into groups, although each group had more or less the same tasks to carry out. The whole class took part in planning the project. The groups were brought together several times for class lessons during the project; at one time they were shown slides of several holiday resorts in different countries and discussed the special features of each one. The teacher was able to reveal information he hoped would be reinforced by the children's own investigations in books and brochures.

Another class lesson was spent discussing the techniques of advertising. The class read extracts from holiday brochures and discussed how the copywriters enticed people to visit certain locations. Work was done on other advertisements and they later tried to write their own for imaginary products. This lesson was deliberately held at a certain point in the project, as the teacher knew that all the children would shortly be designing their own holiday brochures for their chosen resorts.

In a third lesson, the teacher had obtained enough passport application forms for the class. He went through the forms and each child filled one in. This lesson was not originally planned, but children were supposed to fill in these forms as part of their group and individual work. However, the teacher had noticed that the first children to try this had become confused, and so he decided to deal with it on a class basis.

These three lessons include one which focused on content, one which prepared children for skills they would need in the near future, and one which focused on skills that needed reinforcing.

In another project, second year juniors were following up a reading of *Charlotte's Web*, and this resulted in work across several areas of the curriculum. The class were organised into groups, and part of their work involved each group preparing a booklet or wallchart on subtopics such as farmyard animals, spiders, the fairground etc. The rest of the project was done on a class and individual basis with each child having a record sheet of work to be completed. Class lessons were organised, but these tended to be used as stimuli for creative writing and poetry.

More teaching was carried out on a group basis. For example, the group doing work on farmyard animals were shown some slides on this topic, while the rest of the class pursued other work. One group were introduced to curve stitching, and went on to make spiders' webs. This same group was told the story of *Arachne*. Another group were given a lesson on using a reference book after their teacher had noticed that some children in this group did not know how to use the index.

Although this teaching focused on the specific needs of groups, several individuals were also given direct teaching, mostly on skills such as using reference books or finding books in the library.

Incidental teaching
Skills taught during a project can help children to see the purpose of them. I refer to this kind of teaching as incidental because it takes place as a sideline to the main work on the project. This does not mean it is less important, or that it cannot be planned for and, indeed, built

into the project work. During the planning stage of the project, the teacher can deliberately include activities which are likely to provide opportunities for incidental teaching.

To give an example of how this can be done, consider again the project on holidays with third year juniors. The teacher wanted to make sure that the children gained a better grasp of using reference books and also wanted to introduce them to telephone directories. He had therefore ensured that activities involving appropriate skills were included in the project. He had also provided suitable resources for teaching the skills. These resources included six copies of one reference book on countries which were borrowed from other classes and libraries, and several copies of the local *Yellow Pages* directory.

When the children were consulting reference books, the teacher was on the look-out for problems in this area. When he noticed several children who were not completely sure of what to do, he drew them together into a group. He talked to them about finding information in books and asked how they did it. Most of the group could tell him what they *should* do, even though they hadn't done it in practice. He gave out the reference books and suggested they play a game with them. He then called out topics and names and the children attempted to be the first to find them (they soon learned that it was quicker to use the index). The game was repeated on two further occasions to ensure that they had grasped the idea.

Later in the project a group of children were planning how they would obtain holiday brochures. They knew they had to go to travel agencies, but did not know where they were situated in their town. At this point the teacher introduced the *Yellow Pages* directories and explained that these would help. The group found the travel agencies, with the teacher's help, who then suggested playing a game with the directories. He gave them some problems which they had to try to be the first to solve, such as, 'Help, my washing machine has broken down. Who can I call?' or 'I've forgotten my mum's birthday. Where can I buy some flowers after school?' This game subsequently became very popular with the class as a whole, and several children wrote what they called 'Help!' cards to use in the game.

When the class had obtained plenty of holiday brochures, the teacher suggested they each choose one particular holiday and fill in the booking form at the back of the brochure. This gave rise to a great deal of incidental work. The whole class had to calculate the cost of their holiday. This gave them a valuable lesson in reading for small details, as they had to read the small print to find out exactly what the cost of a holiday would be. They discussed items such as insurance and child reductions, and later marked the resorts they had chosen on maps, along with their destination airports.

Only part of this work was fully planned, and clearly a teacher contemplating this approach has to be alert and prepared for teaching opportunities. There is little point in noticing an opportunity for incidental teaching without having the appropriate resources available. The immediacy of the moment is all important. The main point of this approach is that the children understand why they are doing a certain exercise.

Other roles

The other roles which the teacher needs to consider concern the children's involvement and their increasing independence as they pursue their work.

Involving children

It is important that all the children in the class have the opportunity to take part in discussing the aims of the project and making plans, and have experience of as wide a range of tasks as possible. Here are some techniques which can help with this.

Keeping records

Making a record of each child's achievements can, in itself, be a check on children's experiences. If we record that a child has developed a certain skill, he or she must have had experience of that skill. If we have no record, then the child's experience may be lacking. Record-keeping can alert us to where experience needs to be reinforced.

Further records may be kept of those experiences which tend not to be assessed in the way that reading and mathematics skills are. Such a record might include the following activities:
- painting,
- drawing,
- using clay,
- making a collage,
- design,
- model-making,
- using the tape-recorder,
- drama,
- mime,
- interviewing,
- cookery,
- weaving.

With the help of a grid, a child's experience of a particular activity can be ticked off against their name, thus easily showing who has missed out.

Rotating roles

Important roles, such as group leader, group reporter and being a member of the editorial board for the class magazine, could be rotated so that, over a period, every child in the class has a turn at each role. The duties could be arranged so that every child would experience the different types of responsibility.

Group leaders, for example, could be responsible for allocating particular tasks within their group, although they would have to abide by group decisions. They would also keep a record of the progress of each activity. Here is an example of such a record used in a class project on communications. This particular group were doing work on television.

The group reporter could be responsible for reporting back to the class on his or her group's progress. Members of the editorial board would be responsible for the design, collation and production of the class magazine.

Spreading specialists
One of the common features of project work is that children with specialist skills tend to use these a great deal of the time. Children good at art are often asked to do the artwork for display, for example. This can be at the expense of learning other skills and of allowing other children to become as good as the specialist.

One way of using specialist skills and ensuring equal opportunities is to use those with special skills as consultants. Everyone in the class can ask their advice but the specialist should not be allowed to do the activity for anyone else.

Promoting independence
Part of any teacher's task is to make him or herself partially redundant by making the children sufficiently independent to function on their own. This particularly applies to project work.

Many of the essential ideas for this have already been dealt with in previous chapters. Especially important is sharing the goal — setting and planning a project with the children. No-one will learn to make decisions about what they will do if they are not given the opportunity to do so. Also important is giving responsibility for certain parts of the project to specific children.

Of course, there will always be occasions when tasks don't go smoothly.

Group two		
Task	Whose job?	Completed
Graph of favourite TV programmes	Darren, Gary	
Analysis of *Radio Times/TV Times*	Susan, Lee	
Wallchart design and mounting	Avril, Gary	
TV camera section	David, Susan	
History section	Lee, Darren	
Programmes section	Avril, Gary	
Stars section	David, Susan	

Children will sometimes make mistakes, fail to live up to the responsibility they are given and let everybody else down. This is the way of the world, but it is not a sufficient reason to stop trying to make children more independent.

Other methods of encouraging independence may perhaps go against the grain. They can, however, be clearly justified. You could refuse to help children with tasks like finding an item in a book or giving them spellings. You may feel that they should already know these things. It is sometimes hard work to achieve independence and it is important that children should not take the easy way out by asking their teacher's help all the time.

This does *not* mean that you should never help the children. After all you are there to teach. But sometimes being too ready to help can be unproductive. If this view of project work is taken, the teacher is going to be occasionally disappointed with the quality of the end products. Never forget that the process of learning is the main priority and the product is of secondary importance. You may,

however, sometimes need to convince others that standards are not slipping because a child-designed wallchart has some spelling mistakes and is not perfectly mounted.

Self-monitoring

Children should be encouraged to monitor their own work. This will help them to become independent whilst keeping the standard of the end product as high as possible. Specific techniques for doing this will be discussed in more detail in the next chapter. However, self-monitoring needs to be built into the project from the very beginning, and the project organised with this in mind.

If, for example, one of the strategies adopted is to have regular sessions when groups report back on their progress, then these sessions have to take place within the time allocated to the project. Children will need to know what is expected from them in these sessions, and how to give reports.

Chapter Seven

Evaluating the project

If teachers are to claim that teaching through projects is an effective means of instruction, they need to be able to demonstrate this effectiveness. They should be able to evaluate project work and, more especially, to evaluate children's achievements and their development in various areas.

Evaluation is not merely a means of justifying what teachers do. It can also provide teachers with a valuable basis for future teaching. By assessing the achievements, strengths and weaknesses of children doing projects, teachers can plan work which builds on strengths and achievements, and remedies weaknesses.

Evaluation, therefore, has a diagnostic function as well as providing a medium for accountability. Bearing these in mind, teachers need to select appropriate techniques for evaluating children's progress in the various skills that are used in project work.

Evaluate what?

The question of evaluation in project work must relate back to the initial aims of the work. As I have already suggested, the three main areas of aims are the development of concepts, of skills and of attitudes. These areas each have their own problems when it comes to evaluation.

Concepts

As children will, hopefully, be motivated to find out about the topic, we can almost take this type of learning for granted. What cannot be taken for granted, however, is the development of concepts. A concept is usually regarded as a piece of generalised knowledge. Children may learn, for example, about life in Norman, Tudor and Victorian times, and build from this knowledge general ideas about

historical change. Similarly, they may observe that water changes form when boiled or frozen, that paper changes when burnt, and that an iron nail changes when left in the damp. From this knowledge they may build up concepts about chemical and physical change and, from these two related sets of ideas, develop more concepts about the nature of change and cause and effect.

The development of these concepts requires knowledge and practical experience, but it is considerably helped by discussion and teaching which enables children to link together pieces of information. This is more important than merely accumulating snippets of information.

To provide appropriate teaching to help develop concepts, teachers need to be aware of the stages their children have so far reached, and this demands some evaluation. Appropriate activities and levels of discussion can then be provided according to whatever project work is being pursued. Some projects lend themselves more readily to the development of certain concepts, and a balance will need to be achieved over several projects so that as many concepts as possible are covered.

The evaluation of concept development is more difficult than the evaluation of children's knowledge. Knowledge can be assessed by asking children questions, although there is no guarantee, of course, that this knowledge is permanent. Concepts, on the other hand, can only be assessed indirectly.

Skills
Skills are more open to assessment, since they relate to what children actually *do*. I argued in Chapter One that skill development is one of the major aims of project work. It is difficult to imagine how many of the skills outlined earlier could be developed in the primary school if some form of project work is not done.

Let us look at the four categories of skills which can be evaluated.

Investigative skills
This area of skills includes observation, identification, classification, recording and explanation.

Because of their nature they are used in practical situations where children have the facts at their fingertips rather than having to use books or other sources of information. To evaluate correctly, you have to use observation techniques which we will discuss later.

Practical skills
This is an extremely wide area of skills which are not all covered in every project. Three sub-areas we looked at earlier are

skills involved in a range of art and craft techniques, those involved in using particular pieces of apparatus and those involved in presenting work.

With the exception of the last category, in particular, handwriting, the development of these skills tends not to be evaluated very often, or very closely. Many teachers will classify their children as being 'good at art and craft', or not, but few will be more specific and identify particular strengths and weaknesses. A more sophisticated assessment will take into account the context in which something is produced, and the facilities and resources available to help produce it.

Information skills
We defined these skills earlier as:
- defining subject and purpose,
- locating information,
- selecting information,
- organising information,
- evaluating information and
- communicating information.

Evaluating the development of these skills is more difficult than we might imagine.

To assess whether children can find information in a book, or choose the correct item of information to answer a particular question, we cannot rely on a simple answer from the child. It is quite common, however, for children to give the correct answers to this sort of question but, when left to themselves to do the actual tasks, to use quite different and less efficient strategies. Several investigations into children's information skills have found this discrepancy between what children say they would do and what they actually do.

The only way to really evaluate the mastery of these skills is to watch children using them in real situations.

Communication skills
These skills are obviously used throughout the primary curriculum, and not just in project work. However, skills of talking, listening, reading and writing are at the core of project work, and their development needs to be evaluated within its context as well as in other situations.

These skills, especially reading and writing, have traditionally been assessed more than any other skills through formal tests. We will look at the problems of this approach later but at this point it should be noted that communication skills are tools, and as such need to be assessed as they are being used to perform real tasks. Project work provides tasks which require these tools, and so assessment should include this type of work.

Attitudes
This is the most difficult area to assess. Finding out what children really feel, rather than say they feel, poses enormous problems. Any evaluation method will have its weaknesses, and it may be that teachers will have to make do with the best estimate. Yet if the development of positive attitudes to school work and to their peers are worthwhile aims of project work, some way needs to be found, however unreliable, to tell if these aims are being achieved. Children's attitudes to learning, their curiosity, their ability and willingness to work independently, and their attitudes to co-operating with others can all be improved by project work. Evaluation is needed to inform teachers whether this is actually happening.

Methods of evaluation

Talk of evaluation and assessment makes many people think in terms of testing children. Finding methods of evaluation then becomes a search for the right test

to use. There is no room here to debate the role of testing but, with special reference to project work, several points can be made which may have a bearing on other areas of the curriculum.

There are actually very few published tests available which claim to assess most of the skills developed in project work. There are tests for reading, of course, but only one or two limited tests for information skills, and none as far as I am aware for investigative skills. It might be possible to produce tests to check children's memories of facts they have accumulated from project work, but almost impossible to produce a test of conceptual development, which is far more important. By and large, if teachers require tests for project work, they will have to devise their own.

If a test were to be found and administered, it would probably reveal very little about children's abilities to pursue project work, or what they might have learnt in the process. The test might reveal what they were capable of doing on that test, but that would not necessarily be the same as what they were capable of in a different situation. As tests tend to produce stress in children, the results might not even reveal a child's true capabilities. Test situations are, by their very nature, false, and results can give a very unreliable guide to real capabilities.

The fact that tests are unreliable as a means of evaluating project work does not really matter. There are other methods which we will look at. All these methods evaluate children's performance while they are actually doing project work. The work itself is used as a testing vehicle, and so evaluations are a more reliable guide to real abilities.

There are three basic ways to assess children's performance during project work: assess what children produce, observe them while they are working and ask them questions about what they are doing.

Assessing products

Having emphasised that the process of producing work is more important in a project than the product itself, it may seem strange to specify the assessment of the product as a means of evaluation. There are, however, several important markers which can be gleaned from a careful inspection of children's work. If this is combined with other assessment techniques which focus more on the process of project work, an all-round assessment can be built up.

When assessing products there are four considerations to bear in mind:
- An assessment must begin by considering the original aims for the piece of work. Products cannot be judged unless these are taken into account.
- It must take into account the capabilities of the children producing the work. A piece of work may be good for one child, but well below another's capacity.
- The product should be assessed in the light of the intended audience. The only real way of judging this is for the work to be assessed by the intended audience if this is at all possible.
- The assessment should take into account the context in which the work was produced. This includes the resources which were available to the child, the kind of help he or she received, and the time taken to produce the work.

Let us analyse the two pieces of children's work on page 114 in the light of these four considerations.

Intruduction

■ The RWS is My Sheeme to Help Save The ■
WildLife as it needs Saving. My IDea is That
iF People agree with This Paphlet They will
Instead of Just Read about it Do
Somthing About it.

Yours sincerelly
O Birchill

① We May not Mind Very Much About The Hunting of The intelligent and Magestic whale'
we only kill The whale to kill cosmic pots e dogfeed cans e you may say what Have I to worry about It's not me who kills Them If They go extinct its not on My shoulders But it is Here again its only for our pleausuere so we must Help Save Animals who are going rabidly extinct Before They go extinct e that will Be very soon unless we Do somthing e fast.

② Perhaps it Dosent Mean Much to you That Most Flowers will Be extinct when we grow up? I used The word will Be will Be iF we dont do Somthing Fast But we Could do Somthing About it But dont do Somthing now But in the

Future The word should really Have Been COULD Have Be I know There are auganisations all over The world But thats not enough They need all The Help They can get!

③ MayBe We think that the High Prices of Fish e Meat is Just a Passing Fase

2·00 For one Fish
2·20 For e Leg of Lamb

Do you Think That COULD ever Happen
No it could never Happen unless The trade industery got really Bad e The goverment got really greedy, Well This isDifferent we are still Thinking of our selves But in This case we cant Do enything About it.

④ I Dont want to worry you
Thats a Lie I Do want to worry you thousands upon thousands of animals are killed every year e it is our WILD Life Being sloutered.

The World Wildlife Fund

all over the world People are killing and skinning animals. Some animals like the elephants are being killed for there ivory tusks other animals tigers for instance are being killed for the beutiful skins, for bags coats and other things. Whale's are killed for dogmeat, and Perfumes this has been done so many times that the whale has almost become extinct in the past year

whales have been killed for the oily skin.

The eagle is quiet rare it is somtimes found in Scotland. Hunters got to hunt for eagles and steel there eggs. they have the eggs blain e then Sell them this happens to lots of birds and this is the cause of the birds becoming rare. Men get the eggs and lots of the birds eggs are stollen so the eggs can not hatch into chicks.

114

Both pieces were produced with similar aims. As part of a project on the environment, these two third-year juniors read pamphlets from the World Wildlife Fund, and Friends of the Earth about the threat of extinction to certain species of animals. After discussion with their teacher, they (along with four other children) agreed that each would write their own pamphlet about this problem, which would aim not only to give its readers information, but also to encourage them to act. These readers were to be other children in the same class.

With regard to the original aim, it can be seen that only one of these pieces of work really fulfils this. It is written in a direct style which communicates information but also tries to worry its readers. The second piece conveys information, but lacks commitment; its style appears too bland to have real impact.

The writer of the first piece was a boy who rarely shone in school work. From his conversation he was clearly bright and interested in a wide range of subjects, but the work he produced was invariably slip-shod and rarely finished. This piece of work was one of his very best and was given great praise by his teacher.

The girl who wrote the second piece always excelled in her work. She worked conscientiously and was universally regarded by teachers in the school as 'clever'. This piece of work was fairly typical: reasonably tidy and accurate rather than inspired.

Both pieces of work were read by other children in the class. When choosing work for the class display on the project, the children included the first but not the second piece. They commented that the

first piece 'made them angry', but insisted that it be typed on the jumbo typewriter before being displayed, because 'the infants won't be able to read it'.

Both children had similar resources available to them for this work. Both were actually written within one lesson, and were first drafts. Neither child wished to revise what they had written.

The first piece of work has to be read very carefully before its merits are appreciated. It is easy to be put off by the poor presentation and bad spellings, and not to realise that this is, in fact, a remarkable piece of writing. The second piece will often be judged more kindly because it is neater and more accurate, but it is, in fact, much less stimulating.

Observing children

Teachers constantly observe children working. As a result, they make assessments of children's abilities and attitudes, and plan future work. Yet, when asked about their methods of assessment, they will rarely count observation amongst them. Perhaps because observation is so common an activity and seems so subjective, it is very underrated in terms of the assessment information it can provide. Yet it has great potential. Its greatest strength is that it enables assessments to be made while children are actually engrossed in their project work; they do not need to be withdrawn into a special testing situation.

As a means of assessment, observation requires a systematic approach and a means of recording the information gained rather than having to rely on memory.

First of all you have to know exactly what you are looking for. You could list the skills you hope to assess, and prepare a checklist. An alternative approach is to list the activities the children will be doing, and leave space for notes.

Here is a simple checklist for making evaluations of the reading and information skills that children use in a project.

The notes you make can be abbreviated like this:
• has not yet mastered this,
■ almost mastered,
◆ competent.

The problem of a systematic approach still remains. Checklists of this kind

Skill for assessment	Points to look for	Performance
Setting goals	Can child specify aims? Can child specify an audience?	
Defining specific purposes	Can child set questions for investigation? Can child organise work?	
Locating information	Can child find information sources? Can child use these sources?	
Using books	Can child assess appropriate books? Can child find information in books?	
Using appropriate reading strategy	Can child skim, scan, and understand what is read?	
Using information	Can child take notes? Can child present information effectively?	
Evaluation of work	Can child evaluate work? Can child suggest improvements?	

cannot be used for observing all the children in a class at once. Neither is it sensible to rely on remembering things that should be noted down and written up after the event; regular observations of each child should be made. One way of doing this is to focus only on two or three children each day, and deliberately assess their work using the checklists. Over two or three weeks the whole class can be covered, and the process begun again.

However, this is not ideal. Some useful information about children's abilities is bound to be missed. The system does ensure, however, that *all* children, and *all* specific skills can be given regular attention.

Asking questions

Observation is not always sufficient to properly evaluate the way children are thinking about their tasks. To obtain a clearer picture we can ask them questions about how they performed various tasks, or about their thoughts as they did them. There are three types of questions which are useful.

Looking-back questions
These are of the, 'Can you tell me how you did that?' type. They are useful when looking at children's work. Revealing answers may be extracted by comments such as, 'That's very interesting. Where did you find that out?' 'What a lot of information! How did you manage to find it all so quickly', and 'You used the encyclopaedia here. Can you tell me what you did?'.

Looking-forward questions
An example of this is, 'Can you tell me how you will do that?' They require children to think about their actions before they carry them out. It is, of course, possible that because the questions make them think through in advance what they will do, they will actually approach the task in a different way to their original intentions. The question may have a teaching role as well as an enquiring one. Questions such as the following may be found useful: 'When you go to the library to look for that book, can you tell me what you will do?', 'When you've got all the information, how will

117

you organise it', and 'Now, how will you be able to tell which books are useful for your project?'

'Thinking out loud' questions
These are of the type, 'What are you thinking as you are doing that?' They can help children to think about certain tasks explicitly and can show when they are approaching a task in the wrong way. They may include questions like: 'As you make notes from that book, can you tell me why you are choosing those items?' and 'That book seems quite difficult. Can you tell me how you are managing to sort it out?'

A version of the project checklist is given. Each skill area is accompanied by suggested questions to help assessments to be made more quickly.

Involving children

As with other parts of project work, children should take part in evaluating their own work. If children learn to evaluate their work they are more likely to realise where they need to improve, and this will increase the chance of real improvements being made.

Skill for assessment	Questions	PERFORMANCE		
		Good	Average	Poor
Setting goals	What do you want to achieve? What will you produce? Who is it for?			
Defining specific purposes	What do you want to find out? What will you include in the finished product? How will you organise your work?			
Locating information	Where will you get your information? How would you get information beyond books? How will you find the books you want in the library? How do you choose the most useful books?			
Using books	How can you tell whether a book is going to be useful? How do you find the information you want in a book? How can you tell if this book is likely to contain reliable information?			
Using appropriate reading strategy	Can you tell me quickly what this chapter is about? Does it tell you anything about what you want to know?			
Using information	Can you show me the notes you made about this chapter or book? Can you take me through your finished product and explain to me why it is as it is? Have you helped the reader by including a contents/index/bibliography/glossary etc?			
Evaluation of work	Are you satisfied with your finished product? Can you suggest any ways you could have improved it? What will you do with it now?			

Most children will not, of their own accord, make detailed evaluations of their work. They need to be encouraged and guided to do this. One effective technique is to ask them regularly how they performed various tasks, and encourage them to say whether on a second occasion they would do it differently. You could use approaches like this:

- 'You have found out a lot about the invention of television, and you have used several books. Do you think you could have done that any quicker?'
- 'You have finished your wallchart. If you were starting all over again, do you think you would do it in exactly the same way, or would you do anything differently?'
- 'This group has been working together on a model of the airport. Do you think you worked well as a group? How might you have organised things differently?'

With some guidance from the teacher, children might eventually be able to ask each other similar questions.

Another technique is to ask them deliberately for evaluations of their own finished work, whether individual items or whole projects. This can be done informally by asking questions, or the children can be asked to write a few sentences about what they think of their work. This can be open-ended, or more structured. For example, 'Think of three areas you are satisfied with in this work. Think of three areas which you think might be improved'.

When children are thoroughly at ease with the idea of criticising their own work, they can be asked, perhaps in small groups, to criticise their classmates' work. The criticisms should not become too negative, or they may damage other children's self-esteem. Phrase the task in such a way that they should suggest ways the work might be improved, rather than simply say what is wrong with it.

Another way to develop self-evaluation is by the regular report-back session which was suggested earlier. One child from each group could give a brief report to the rest of the class on how the group's project work is progressing. The reporter can be encouraged to mention any problems the group have had, anything they are particularly proud of, or any areas in which they are not sure how to proceed and would really appreciate some help. The group's problems could then be discussed by the whole class, and suggestions made as to how they might be overcome. In this way, a co-operative, 'help each other' atmosphere can be encouraged.

Record keeping

Teachers are regularly told that they should keep records of progress in all areas of the curriculum. The golden rule of record-keeping, however, is simply this: **if records are not consulted and used as a guide for future teaching, then there is no point in making them in the first place.**

Records should not be kept for their own sake, but only if they actually assist the process of teaching. With a limited amount of time available to teachers, records have to be economic in terms of the time taken to compile them, and also in the time needed to consult and draw upon them. Most will require only one or two word comments.

Name: Darren Taylor   Year: Junior 2

Project	Major activities
Vikings	Story writing, drama, model-making, using reference books, map-making.
Water	Science experiments, collage, editor of class magazine, visit to reservoir, designed school questionnaire.

Name: Darren Taylor   Year: Junior 2

Area	Comment on progress
Skills:	
Investigative	Able to observe quite carefully and discuss and classify observations. Recording still rather weak.
Practical	Presentation quite poor. Excellent design.
Information	Use of reference books improving. Planning is good. More consideration needs to be given to presenting information.
Communication	Reading for information good. Can explain ideas well but has difficulty in written expression.
Attitudes	Very positive towards learning and information. Co-operates well, but needs help to become more independent in his work.
General conceptual development	Has begun to understand historical change. Needs more experience to grasp cause and effect, especially in science work. Finds it difficult to approach tasks systematically.

As far as project work is concerned, there are two types of useful records. The first is of the experiences and areas children have covered, and the second is a record of their development in particular areas, for example, skills.

Experience records

I have already suggested that the problem of continuity in project work might be alleviated by keeping records of the project area covered, and the main work experiences children have had. If a teacher knows the projects children have already covered, he or she might still choose to repeat and extend any of them, but at least this would be done with deliberate purpose, rather than by accident. A simple record like the one given here might accompany individual children through the school.

Achievement records

These may exist in two forms. Firstly there should be a record for individual teachers' use. This needs to be fairly detailed so that the teacher can use it as a basis for planning work. Secondly there needs to be a record to pass on to the child's next teacher. This will probably not have the same level of detail, but will be more of a summary of the child's main strengths and weaknesses. An example of this second kind of record is given here:

A record for class teachers to use needs to be more detailed, and should be broken down into finer categories. Simpler forms of recording information will probably be adopted, using ticks or crosses, or classifications like 'Good', 'Average' or 'Poor'. There is, however, a lot to be gained by keeping clearer and more detailed records if you have the time.

Appendix

Appendix

Stories and poems

All those listed below make useful starting points for project work.

Novels
Charlotte's Web E B White (Puffin).
The Iron Man: A Story in Five Nights Ted Hughes (Faber).
The Sea Egg Lucy Boston (Puffin).
The Third Class Genie Robert Leeson (Collins).
James and the Giant Peach Roald Dahl (Puffin).
A Dog So Small Philippa Pearce (Puffin).

Short Stories
The Fantastic Machine Barry Maybury, in *Bandwagon* Barry Maybury (ed) (Oxford University Press).
How the Whale Became and Other Stories Ted Hughes (Young Puffin).
The Elephant's Petals Brian Patten, in *Bandstand* Barry Maybury (ed) (Oxford University Press).
A Hamster at Large Philippa Pearce in *The Red Storyhouse* David Jackson and Dennis Pepper (eds) (Oxford University Press).

Lion at School Philippa Pearce in *The Yellow Storyhouse* David Jackson and Dennis Pepper (eds) (Oxford University Press).
Spit Nolan, in *The Goalkeeper's Revenge and Other Stories* Bill Naughton (Puffin).
The Fib in *The Fib and Other Stories* George Layton (Armada Lions)

Poems
The Tail of the Trinosaur Charles Causley (Beaver Books) *(op)*.
The Pied Piper of Hamelin Robert Browning, in *The Faber Book of Children's Verse* (Faber & Faber).
The Lion and Albert Marriott Edgar (Methuen).
The Golden Vanity and *Lord Randal*, in *I'll Tell You a Tale* Ian Serraillier (Kestrel).
The Marrog R C Scriven, in *Bandstand* Barry Maybury (ed) (Oxford University Press.

Two useful series of books are:
Bandstand, Bandwagon, Wordscapes, Thoughtshapes, Thoughtweavers, and *Wordspinners* edited by Barry Maybury (Oxford University Press); and *The Storyhouse* Series by David Jackson and Dennis Pepper (Oxford University Press).
op   Book is out of print; try libraries.

Teaching children to use books

Some suggestions for teaching how to use the library and its books are given below.

Using the library

Teach the children how and why a library organises its information books. To do this you will need a large box containing around 30 information books, including three or four each on the Romans and birds.

Suggest there are two major reasons for using a library: leisure reading (stories, hobbies, general interest etc and information (facts you want to find). For example, finding a book to identify a bird is a hobby, but discovering what a Roman soldier wore is usually for homework or a project.

The aim of this lesson is to show how a library organises its information books so that people can find books themselves. Begin by finding out how some of the children organise their books at home.

Ask the children:
• Who has books at home?
• How many books?
• Where are they kept?
• Can you find what you want?
• Do they need to be put in a special order?

Answers will show that children don't keep their books in any order because they do not have many books, or because not many people use them. Ask them why this would not work in a large library.

Get the children to look at books in school or a public library, and ask them:
• How many books are there in this library?
• Could you remember all their titles?
• Do you know where the books on atoms are kept?
• Do you know where the books on magnetism are kept?
• Do you know where books on crochet are kept?

Explain that where there are large numbers of books, and a lot of people using them, we must organise the books so that everyone can find what they want.

The children should be encouraged to think for themselves how information books could best be arranged. Take them step by step through an imaginary situation where there is no organisation of books.

Ask them to imagine that:

- All the books in the library are thrown into one huge box. How would a book on birds or Romans be found?
- Using a large box and 30 or so pre-selected books, ask two children to find one book on Romans and one book on birds. Each book has to be taken out in turn until the right one is found.
- Ask for suggestions to make it easier to find books on particular topics. Then get the children to put all bird books from the box in one pile on the floor, and put all the books on Romans in another pile. They should then arrange all the remaining books from the box into different subject piles. Do they find that:
- It is easier to see where certain books are kept?
- Can they see everything the library has on each topic?

They will realise that this is more organised than having the books jumbled in the box, but there is still the problem of finding the right pile. A library contains hundreds of subjects, which would mean hundreds of piles of books.

Select ten subjects, covering three main areas, such as countries, history, and nature, and show the illustration to the children. Ask for suggestions to improve the arrangement of the piles.

Could any of the piles be grouped together? Are there any piles on the same *kind* of subjects?

Finally, show the subjects grouped together in three main areas, and explain that it is now quicker to find a book on a subject because:

- They will know in which group the subject is kept,
- They will only have a few piles of books to search through,
- In one subject pile they will find *all* the books in the library on that subject.

The library arranges its books in the same way, but the books are on the shelves, not in piles on the floor. Books on the same subject are put together and books on similar subjects are kept close to each other.

Using a book

Using a reference book can be a daunting task to many children, but helping them with the first step, which is learning how to use the contents pages of an information book, will give them the confidence to make a start. Provide the class with six copies of a reference book suitable for the children's abilities.

Get the children to look at the various parts of the book. Point out the contents page and ask what its purpose is. It does, in fact, have two:

- it gives a general outline of topics covered in the book, and
- it tells you where to find particular topics in the book.

Ask the children questions such as: 'Who can be the first to tell me which chapter is about . . . ?' Try to grade the questions so that they become less and less obvious. For example, if the contents page mentions a chapter called 'The Egyptians', one of the first questions might be, 'Which chapter tells us about people who lived in Egypt?' A later question might be, 'Which chapter might mention the Pyramids?'

Finish by asking questions to which there might be more than one answer. Discuss what to do in these circumstances.

Resources

Directions J Cooper (Oliver & Boyd). Six books which concentrate on reading skills.

Primary Language Course (study skills Level 1 and 4) C Cuff (Cambridge Educational).

Reading Skills and Reference Work P Smith (Macmillan Education).

Research Skills James McCafferty (Edward Arnold). Includes three workbooks and teachers' book.

Targets: Reading Skills for Learning D Brogden (Nelson). Five books, including introductory book.

Study Reading C Burgess (Schofield & Sims). Modules E-K and teachers' book.

Working with Information C Burgess (Schofield & Sims). Six books.